Richard Garnett

Richmond on the Thames

Richard Garnett

Richmond on the Thames

ISBN/EAN: 9783337733063

Printed in Europe, USA, Canada, Australia, Japan

Cover: Foto ©ninafisch / pixelio.de

More available books at **www.hansebooks.com**

RICHMOND ON THE THAMES

BY

RICHARD GARNETT, C.B., LL.D.
KEEPER OF THE PRINTED BOOKS IN THE BRITISH MUSEUM

LONDON
SEELEY AND CO., LIMITED, ESSEX STREET, STRAND
NEW YORK: MACMILLAN AND CO.
1896

LIST OF ILLUSTRATIONS

PLATES

	PAGE
Richmond Hill. Etched by John Fullwood, R.S.B.A.	*Frontispiece*
The Thames, from the Buccleugh Gardens. Etched by Clough Bromley	48
The View from Richmond Hill. By G. Barrett, jun. Engraved by T. Huson, R.P.E.	56
Richmond Bridge. By Turner. Engraved by T. Huson, R.P.E.	68

ILLUSTRATIONS IN THE TEXT

The Palace, Richmond. From an old Engraving	10
The Palace, Richmond. From the Etching by W. Hollar, 1638	11
Richmond Hill and the Palace in the Seventeenth Century. After a Picture by Vinckenboom in the Fitzwilliam Museum, Cambridge	13
Henry VII. From the Effigy by Torrigiano in Westminster Abbey	17
The Palace of Richmond. From an Engraving by Buck, 1737	24
Remains of the Palace, Richmond. Drawn by Clough Bromley	26
Richmond Lodge. From a Water-colour Drawing in the Crace Collection, British Museum	31
Thomson's Summer-house. From an Engraving by W. B. Cooke, after G. Barnard	37
Richmond Church. Drawn by Clough Bromley	39
Sir Joshua Reynolds' House on Richmond Hill. By J. Farrington, R.A. Engraved by T. Huson, R.P.E.	40
The View from Richmond Hill. By Sir Joshua Reynolds. Engraved by T. Huson, R.P.E.	41
The Thames and Richmond Hill, from the Earl of Cholmondeley's House, 1749	43
Richmond Theatre. From an old Engraving. Reproduced by T. Huson, R.P.E.	46
Richmond Park Gate. By J. Brown, 1805	51

LIST OF ILLUSTRATIONS

	PAGE
The White Lodge, Richmond Park. Drawn by Clough Bromley	53
The White Lodge, Richmond Park, in the time of Lord Sidmouth	55
In Richmond Park looking towards Petersham. Drawn by Clough Bromley	57
The Terrace, Richmond. Drawn by Clough Bromley	59
View from Richmond Hill. By P. De Wint	61
The View from Richmond Hill. By Turner. Reproduced from the Engraving by J. T. Wilmore, by T. Huson, R.P.E.	63
Richmond Hill and the old Star and Garter. By J. D. Harding. Engraved by T. Huson, R.P.E.	65
The old Star and Garter. From a Drawing by Captain Grose, British Museum. Engraved by T. Huson, R.P.E.	67
The Ferry, with Richmond Lodge in the distance. After Marco Ricci. Engraved by T. Huson, R.P.E.	71
The Duke of Buccleugh's Cottage, 1832; now the Residence of Sir J. Whittaker Ellis, Bart. By G. Barnard. Engraved by T. Huson, R.P.E.	73
The Thames from the Duke of Buccleugh's Garden. By W. Westall, A.R.A. Engraved by T. Huson, R.P.E.	75
The Thames and Twickenham Eyot. By T. M. Baynes, 1823. Engraved by T. Huson, R.P.E.	77
Richmond Bridge, from Isleworth Meadows. After R. R. Reinagle, R.A.	81
The Old Palace at Kew. By Paul Sandby, R.A.	83
Kew Gardens in the Eighteenth Century. By W. Woollett	87
Palace at Kew built by George III. By W. Daniell, R.A.	88
Kew Green. Drawn by Clough Bromley	90
Petersham Church. Drawn by Clough Bromley	91
Ham House. Drawn by Clough Bromley	92
Pope's House, Twickenham. From an old Engraving	95
Twickenham Church. From a Print by G. W. Pickett. Reproduced by T. Huson, R.P.E.	97
Strawberry Hill. By Paul Sandby, R.A. Engraved by T. Huson, R.P.E.	99
The Gallery, Strawberry Hill. From an old Engraving. Reproduced by T. Huson, R.P.E.	100

CHAPTER I

THE OLD PALACE AND MONASTERIES

> Not wholly in the busy world, nor quite
> Beyond it, blooms the garden that I love.

THESE lines of the poet express the sentiment which has always guided monarchs, statesmen, and others engaged in the practical business of the world, in the selection of retreats from the cares of government and business. Hence some of the most delightful spots on earth are found in the vicinity of great cities, where taste has taken advantage of natural beauty, and converted fields and woods into parks and gardens. It may be, however, that the world has now seen almost the last of such *rura in urbe*. Two causes militate strongly against their perpetuation —the vast increase in the dimensions of modern cities, so infinitely beyond anything that could have been anticipated in past ages, and the still less expected acceleration of the means of transit, which now enables recreation to be sought at considerable distances without relaxing the sovereign's or the statesman's hold upon public affairs. Henry VII., the second founder of Richmond and the bestower of its present appellation, had a palace at Greenwich also. No place could have seemed more appropriate for the residence of the sovereign of a great marine state, on the way to be the first sea-power in the world ; and there, in fact, Queen Elizabeth by preference received foreign ambassadors. By the time of Charles II., however, residence there had become impossible even to a less pleasure-loving sovereign, and only the happy thought of Nell Gwynne (if it was hers) has preserved Greenwich as an object of national pride and interest. Richmond has suffered less.

It will appear from the following pages how the creation of the park, and of the gardens of the adjacent Kew, while in a measure encouraging residence, have protected it from being utterly swamped by suburban extension and merely utilitarian encroachments. Yet its royal days are over; its warmest admirers must acknowledge that the Sovereign is more fitly established at Windsor, and that, should any change occur, it will rather be in the direction of greater remoteness from, than closer proximity to the capital. Its destiny in the future is that of a retreat and playground for the people, especially for the metropolis, and great will be their shame and loss if they suffer it to be spoiled either by the sinister interests or the meddlesome interference which are always conspiring against the beautiful.

The particular qualification of Richmond for the country retreat of a great city is tersely expressed in a line of Thomson's celebrated description :

> Where the silver Thames first rural grows.

The particular wording is a little odd. Thomson seems to think that a river grows like a tree, from the widest part upwards. It would have been more correct to have said that below Richmond the silver stream grows suburban. The general proposition, however, is correct; and if we inquire why the demarcation between the poetry and the prose of the river should be thus marked at this point, the answer may be given in two words—Richmond Hill. The peculiar favour of Nature has here adorned the generally level banks of the stream with an eminence from which their beauties can be contemplated with a consummate felicity which could not have been surpassed if the site had been the choice, and the hill the creation, of the most accomplished human taste; and man has not been backward in accepting the hint and embellishing the ground to an extent which it may be hoped will preserve it as a spot for ever sacred from disfigurement. By whom its beauty was first remarked cannot be told.[1] The sites of Roman villas are usually distinguished for the picturesqueness of the view they command, and as

---

[1] To avoid perpetual acknowledgments of indebtedness, we state once for all our obligations to Manning and Bray's *Surrey*, and to the histories of Richmond by Mr. Crisp and Mr. Chancellor.

London was a flourishing city in imperial times, Richmond Hill is just the place where such a residence might have been expected. We are not aware, however, that any Roman remains have been found there. The appreciation of the Anglo-Saxon would be certain if the first name by which Richmond appears in history—Shene (still preserved as the name of an adjacent hamlet), could be connected, as all historians and topographers do connect it, with the Saxon *scine*, shining or beautiful. But it is a safe rule to distrust the etymology which first offers itself as plausible. Whether the word is to be taken as a substantive or as an adjective, whether it is to be understood as referring to the verdant lustre of the scenery, or, as Camden will have it, to the splendour of the royal palaces erected on the spot, the derivation is equally alien to the genius of the language, and there can be little doubt that the name is a corruption of some term not yet traced. It may even be Norman, since the word does not occur in any Anglo-Saxon document : neither does it appear in Domesday Book ; but in a Harleian manuscript, said to be of nearly equal antiquity, Shene is spelt *Syene*, which suggests that the adjoining Syon Convent, the predecessor of Syon House, may not have been originally named after Mount Sion. It is probably a token of the more settled condition to which England had attained under Henry I. that he is the first monarch known to have possessed a residence at Shene, his Norman predecessors having been kept continually on the move by wars and commotions. It probably was little more than a country house; for, some time after his death, the manor and appurtenances appear to have been granted to John Belet, the king's cup-bearer. It may well be believed that Stephen, whose reign was a continuous battle when he was not actually in captivity, found little time or inclination to enjoy the rural beauties of Shene. Belet's family became extinct in the male line in the reign of Henry III., and, after various vicissitudes, the manor reverted to the Crown in the reign of Edward I., who undoubtedly made it a royal residence, and must in all probability be regarded as the original founder of a royal palace on the spot. The date of erection was probably between 1292, when the Bishop of Bath and Wells died possessed of the manor of Shene, and 1305, when, according to Matthew of Westminster, Edward received there the Scottish nobles who came to treat with him after the execution of William Wallace. The dates of various documents show that Edward II. occasionally resided at Shene; and it was an especially favourite residence with Edward III., who died there on June 21, 1377, having only a few days previously received in it the French commissioners who came to treat of peace. It was therefore within the precincts of Shene that the painful scene occurred, if it really did occur, of the king's desertion by his mistress, Alice Perrers, who, finding his condition desperate, is said to have drawn the rings off his fingers and left him. The truth of the story, however, and indeed the nature of the king's relations with Alice, are matters involved in much uncertainty. The preference which Edward had manifested for Shene was for a time even more marked under his successor, Richard II., who greatly enlarged and beautified it, and was making it more and more of a royal residence, when his affection for it was converted into distaste by the death within its walls of his idolised consort, Anne of Bohemia, June 7, 1394. In the transport of his grief Richard is said to have commanded the palace to be pulled down. Such a proceeding would be entirely in keeping with the impulsive, mutable, affectionate and at the same time irascible temperament which Shakespeare, of whose own universal character similar feelings were not the least important constituents, has so marvellously represented in his tragedy on the fate of this interesting and most unhappy sovereign. There seems, however, no sufficient authority for the statement, which probably grew out of the dilapidated condition into which the palace fell after its desertion by both Richard and his successor, Henry IV. It was rebuilt by Henry V., whose biographer, Elmham, describes his edifice as "a delightful mansion, of curious and costly workmanship, and befitting the character and condition of a king." The dates of some official documents show that Henry VI. was residing here in 1441 and 1442, and in 1456, upon his becoming incapacitated for government, and the disturbances occasioned by the pretensions of Richard Duke of York, he was sent to Shene for quiet and security. Edward IV. kept court here in 1465, and in the following year granted it to his queen, Elizabeth Woodville, for her life; and here the princesses were educated under the tuition of Lady Berners.

The fifteenth century, intellectually one of the poorest periods in the history of England, was materially one of great development. The early years of Henry VI., indeed, are revealed by the Paston Letters as a time of great confusion and disorganisation from the weakness of the Government and the lawlessness and rapacity of strong-fisted barons; and the situation apparently became much worse during the anarchy and bloodshed of the ensuing civil wars. The evil, nevertheless, worked out its own cure by the destruction of the old feudal system and most of the old hereditary families as a consequence of these wars, and the room thus afforded for the development of the new forces that had been silently growing up. A middle class emerged from the chaos, with increased wealth, comparative culture, greatly enhanced standards of comfort, and, in general, with the ideals and aspirations of the modern age. One of the most evident external tokens of the new spirit was the gradual disappearance or dilapidation of the old castellated strongholds, now no longer necessary as fortresses, and obsolete and inconvenient as dwellings. The moated hall, a compromise between the castle and the country house, takes their place; and though the knight remains an influential member of society, his military character merges itself more and more in his character as country gentleman. Speaking roughly, the new era may be said to have come in with the accession of Edward IV., whose policy it was to rely more upon the new nobility than the old, and upon the citizens than either. The complete extinction of civil strife under Henry VII. was exceedingly favourable to these tendencies. In his reign the new spirit becomes unquestionably dominant, and it is symbolised in a striking way by the change which Shene underwent at his hands. What improvements and extensions it may have received at the beginning of his reign cannot now be known, but they were no doubt considerable, as three years after his accession we find the Court spending Whitsuntide there, and in May 1492 Shene is the place of "a great and valiant justing, the which endured by the space of a moneth," and was attended by what would in these days be considered a highly sensational circumstance. A controversy having arisen between Sir James Parker and Hugh Vaughan respecting a coat of arms granted to the latter, which was probably thought to encroach upon the former's privileges, the matter was referred to the arbitrament of a tilt, which was decided in Vaughan's favour in the most conclusive manner by the giving way of his antagonist's helmet, "and so he was striken into the mouth, that his tongue was borne into the hinder part of his head, and so he died incontinently." The festivities had been preceded by a solemn thanksgiving for the expulsion of the Moors from Spain, and probably had a connection with that

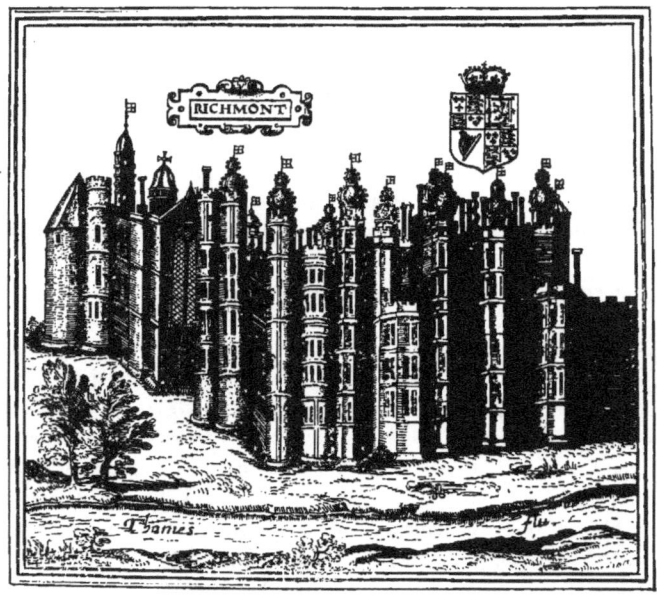

The Palace, Richmond.   From an old Engraving.

event. A treaty had already been concluded between England and Spain at Medina del Campo on March 27, 1489, providing among other things for the marriage of the Prince of Wales and the Princess Catherine of Aragon, afterwards so closely connected with England and Shene.

The great glory of Shene, and the acquisition of the name by which it is now known, were nevertheless mainly owing to what might have been an irremediable calamity. One December night, the royal palace,

The Palace, Richmond. From the Etching by W. Hollar, 1638.

at which Henry was then residing, was almost wholly destroyed by fire. The date usually assigned for this catastrophe is 1497, but this seems impossible, for in Mr. Bergenroth's *Calendar of the State papers relating to negotiations between England and Spain* is a letter from the Spanish ambassador De Puebla, dated July 15, 1498, stating that the king has invited him to *Xin*, and two days afterwards is another letter actually dated from the place. It is clear, therefore, that Henry was then living at Shene. Another letter, from Henry himself, is dated Shene, June 1599, 14; and no further mention of the place occurs until 25th September 1501, when Henry writes from it under its new name of RICHMOND. The date of 1499, assigned to the disaster by Mr. Crisp, is therefore in all probability correct. The name of Richmond was, as universally known, conferred by Henry upon Shene in memory of the title which he had himself borne before he came to the crown, and was derived from the town of Richmond in Yorkshire. He could not well have given the place of his predilection a stronger token of his regard, and the splendour of the buildings he erected appears to have been in strong contrast with his habitual parsimony. A manuscript, written in 1503, and printed in Grose and Astell's *Antiquarian Repertory*, gives a glowing account of the structure, "girded and encompassed with a strong and mighty brick wall, barred and bent with towers in his each corner and angle and also in his midway. His openings be strong gates of double timber and heart of oak, stuck full of nails right thick, and crossed with bars of iron." The writer proceeds to dilate upon the courtyard, the windows looking upon it, and the chambers to which they belong, and describes particularly the great hall with portraits of the kings of England between the windows, including "our most excellent and high sovereign" Henry himself; also "the rich cloths of arras," representing many noble battles and sieges. The "decent and pleasant chapel" is particularly described, and must assuredly have presented a glowing picture with its hangings of arras and cloth of gold, the gold and jewels encrusted in the altar, the emblazoned ceiling, and the mural paintings of such kings as were also saints. The other rooms are glanced at, down to the scullery; and the garden is said to be "with many vines, seeds, and strange fruit right goodly beset." Mention is also made of the arbours and summer-houses with

Richmond Hill and the Palace in the Seventeenth Century. *After a Picture by Vinckenboom in the Fitzwilliam Museum.*

provision for playing chess, tables, and cards; also of bowling alleys, archery grounds, and tennis courts. One of the quaintest remarks relates to the vanes on the towers, which are declared to be equally pleasant to see and hear upon a windy day. Very little of this splendour, it will be seen, remained when the Parliamentary Commissioners made their report in the seventeenth century. The disappearance of furniture and tapestry is easily understood, but it must be feared that the mural paintings had been submerged under coats of whitewash.

The views of the palace engraved for this monograph afford an excellent idea of its appearance, both as originally erected for Henry VII. and of its external condition in the early part of the seventeenth century. It is especially interesting as a Tudor structure, for, being entirely the erection of Henry VII. himself, and not formed by adapting or repairing any edifice already existing, it is an accurate index to the architectural taste of the time in domestic architecture, when the sole determining factors were pleasure and convenience. It may be taken to represent the best ideal that, outside the domain of military and ecclesiastical architecture, the taste of the time was capable of forming, and we see with pleasure that picturesqueness must have been regarded as an essential element in architecture. This object was fully attained by judicious colouring, oblong or diamond shaped patches of black brick having been originally superimposed upon a ground of warm red; by the variety of the outline, where the monotony of the level frontage is broken up by the intermixture of semicircular towers sallying forward from the background; by fine mullioned windows; but especially by the forest of turrets, which could have had no other than a picturesque motive. These offer a strong affinity to the Saracenic type of architecture, which may well have influenced English taste through our then close connection with Spain, and are indeed by no means unlike in outline to the Egyptian mosque-lamps, which form at the present day the joy of the collector of ancient glass. In the neighbouring palace of Hampton Court, built by Cardinal Wolsey twenty years later, the same type appears in a more chastened form. The chief drawback to the generally good effect of the building is its huddled appearance, arising principally from the narrowness of the projecting towers and the manner in which they are crowded together upon a not too extensive front. This impression is assisted by the close proximity of the palace to the river, and the blank prosaic style of its location on the bare ground without apparent relief, except from the slight embankment at the water's edge and the raised terrace-walk. It appears to far more advantage in the other views we have engraved, the drawing by Hollar dated 1638, and the fine old picture attributed to Vinckenboom, which, from the details of costume, appears to be of about the same period. In these, provided with a foreground and a background, and shown, as it actually appeared, in due connection with the surrounding accessories which contributed to make up the entire picture, it appears as the dominant figure in a landscape of extreme beauty, and we have only to reproduce to the mind's eye the freshness and colour of the landscape, the blue or silver of the rippling river, the green of the trees and pastures, the varying tints of the sky against which its pinnacles were outlined, the gliding boats and picturesque costumes, to imagine the charm of the scene for the visitor under the Tudors or the early Stuart sovereigns.

Abundant testimony continues to occur of the fame Richmond enjoyed among royal palaces, and the frequent residence of the sovereign. In 1501 the marriage contract between Prince Arthur and Princess Catherine of Aragon was concluded there, and after the Prince's death in the ensuing year it was assigned to his widow as a residence, and her letters are frequently dated from it until the death of Henry in 1509. He frequently appears as residing there himself, especially in 1506, when Philip, King of Castile, having been driven to England by a storm, was entertained for a considerable time at Richmond. Henry himself died there on April 21, 1509, "in great calm of a consuming sickness." Selfish and avaricious, void of honour and even decency in his crooked political intrigues, this prudent monarch nevertheless conferred great benefits upon his kingdom, among which may be justly enumerated his care for the beautiful domain which his parsimony might have induced him to alienate. The entries in his book of privy expenses seem to indicate that he kept some kind of a menagerie, and he is said to have deposited here some of the jewels in which he invested a portion of the cash which he wrung by taxation from his subjects, for their own good, as he explained to the Spanish Ambassador. They would, he said, become disorderly if they were too well off. He did not think with

Cobbett that money should be left "to fructify in the pockets of the people."

Henry VII. and his successor not unnaturally became the subjects of legend, thus narrated by Friedrich Gerschen, who, in 1602, visited Richmond in the retinue of the Duke of Pomerania :—

"There were here manuscripts highly valued by *Henricus Octavus*: among them were many curious things, amongst others a round mirror in which the king was said to see everything, and it was almost believed he

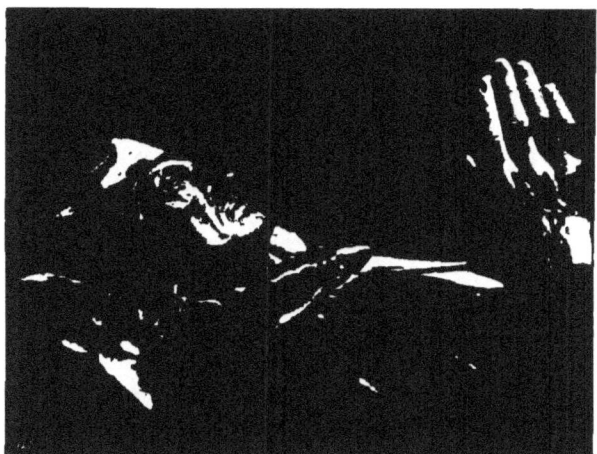

Henry VII. From the Effigy by Torrigiano in Westminster Abbey.

had a *spiritum familiarem* sitting in it, for the mirror broke to pieces the moment after the king's death. This king commanded that after his death his entrails should be taken out of his body and thrown three times against the wall, which gave rise to many strange rumours. Some say it was done out of great devotion. I reserve my *judicium* and opinion about the mirror. We saw the apartment in which he expired, also the three bloody marks on the wall, caused by fulfilling his last wish.

"In the apartment next to it, the above king's father kept a great treasure secretly hidden under the floor, and made his servant, to whom he confided it, swear not to reveal anything about this money to *Henricus Octavus*, whose behaviour was rather wild, unless some great distress should befall the realm. As, however, after his father's death the son took to his *studia* with great diligence, the servant showed him the place, and this said treasure was spent in obtaining the costly tapestries in Hampton Court and the royal houses."

It will have occurred to the judicious reader that the German traveller has committed a slight mistake, for *Henricus Octavus* did not die at Richmond, but at Westminster. In fact, the curious stories about the sprinkling of the walls with blood, and the magic glass—the latter also related of the Egyptian king, Nectanebus, and other renowned magicians—do not concern him, but Henry VII., as unanimously attested by other German travellers, collected in Mr. W. B. Rye's learned and entertaining *England as seen by Foreigners*; Grasser, 1606; Zingerling, 1610; and Eisenberg, 1614. Grasser tells us that the mirror was circular, and does not say that it was broken in his time; but this is distinctly stated by the other travellers. All mention having seen the blood-stains on the wall, which, though no English authority mentions them, no doubt existed; although the cause assigned for their origin is without question legendary, and was probably invented to account for their appearance. The tale of the hidden treasure is peculiar to Gerschen; it is perhaps connected with the remarkable piece of information imparted by Grasser, that "the secret passages used by this king were first discovered under Queen Elizabeth." A legend, not mentioned by the German travellers, that Henry VIII. beheld from an eminence near Richmond the rockets which announced the execution of Anne Boleyn, is refuted by the simple circumstance that Anne was decapitated at nine in the morning. Miss Strickland gets rid of the absurdity of the story by changing the rockets into a gun. But it is demonstrable that the king must have been on that day at Wolf Hall in Wiltshire. The story doubtless arose from the fact of a knoll in Lord Errol's grounds, adjoining the park, an ancient tumulus, being locally known as "The King's Standing," a name which it probably obtained from Charles I., the creator of the park.

The death of Henry VII. did not diminish the favour in which Richmond was held by royalty. Henry VIII. kept Christmas there in 1509, the year of his accession. On New Year's Day, 1511, a prince was born at Richmond who only lived seven weeks, and but for whose decease the divorce of Queen Catherine might never have taken place, and the Reformation might only have been effected at the cost of a tremendous civil war. At Richmond, in 1522, the Emperor Charles V., whose retinue overtaxed the resources of the Palace, was entertained with extraordinary magnificence. Shortly afterwards it was granted as a residence to Wolsey, who had sought to appease the king's jealousy by resigning his own palace of Hampton Court to him. Wolsey displayed his usual magnificence in his new abode, but his occupation was short, although after his fall he was permitted to live for a time at the Lodge in Richmond Park, which had been a short time previously built and occupied by Dean Colet. Here both Anne Boleyn and Jane Seymour came; and after the divorce of Anne of Cleves she received the palace for her residence, but does not appear to have lived there very long, as it was frequently occupied by Edward VI., who preferred it to Windsor, where, he said, he always felt like a prisoner. Mary lived there shortly after her accession, and there spent the greater part of the miscalled honeymoon of her unhappy marriage. Shortly afterwards the palace became a prison, being appointed the residence of the Princess Elizabeth, then under virtual restraint; but who, after her reconciliation with her sister, came up by water as a guest, and was received with apparent rejoicing. In the following year (1558) Mary was again at Richmond, and the proximate cause of her death was thought to have been a chill contracted there from the inclemency of the summer.

Considerable light is thrown upon the internal arrangements of Richmond Palace in Queen Mary's time by a curious document—a letter written from Rigamonte (Richmond), August 17, 1554, by one of the Spanish gentlemen in the suite of Philip II., who had just come over to attend his master upon his marriage, and was then lodged in the palace.[1] "All entertainment here," he says, "is eating and drinking, for they have no notion of any other. The Queen spends more than three hundred thousand ducats a year on victual; and all the thirteen Lords of Council, and the officers of the Queen's household, and the King's household officers (who are English), and the wives of all these, have their meals in the palace;

[1] Edited along with the narration of Andres Muñoz by Señor Pascual de Gayangos. Madrid, 1887.

and so have the ladies-in-waiting, and their servants, and everybody else's servants, and two hundred guards. All these ladies and gentlemen sleep and have their apartments in the palace, and every one knows his own room. Every lord has a cook of his own in the Queen's kitchen, and there are eighteen kitchens beside; and so great is the bustle that every kitchen seems a piece of the infernal regions. And so, though the palaces are so large that the least of the few we have seen is larger and has more and bigger rooms than the citadel of Madrid, there are so many people to be lodged that it is hardly possible to find room for them all.

"From eighty to a hundred sheep are usually consumed every day in the palace, and the sheep here are very big. They also consume daily a dozen head of cattle, also very large; and a dozen and a half of calves, to say nothing of what comes from the chase—venison, boars (?), and quantities of rabbits. They drink more beer than there comes down water at Valladolid in a spring flood. The ladies and some of the gentlemen put sugar into their wine. And there is very great racket and rumpus in the palace. And though there are so many rooms they have never given one to the Duchess of Alva. They are the most ungrateful people that ever were seen, and would just as soon see the devil as a Spaniard. There are so many thieves among them that these go about by twenties. They have no justice, and no fear of God. Mass is seldom said, and those who attend it do so against their will, except where the Queen is, for she is a holy woman and fears God. For us there is no justice; we are admonished from His Majesty to raise no question about anything, but to put up with everything as long as we are in the country."

Hence, although passing a hearty eulogium on the natural beauties of England, which, he says, exactly confirm the descriptions in the romances of chivalry, our Spaniard concludes by declaring that it will be a blessed day when he finds himself back in Flanders; in which sentiment English people, we may be sure, entirely coincided with him.

The favour which Mary had shown to Richmond was even more conspicuously displayed by Elizabeth, who not only frequently resided there but kept a brilliant court. She was there in 1564, 1565, and 1567, and in 1581 selected it as the place of the entertainment of the ambassadors of the Duke of Anjou, with whom she was carrying on one of the numerous insincere flirtations that distressed their objects and her own subjects, but no doubt favoured her political schemes. A banqueting hall was erected at a cost of £1200, and all was pomp and amusement. It was at Richmond on October 11, 1581, that Elizabeth gave the Spanish ambassador the remarkable audience at which she addressed him "with terrible insolence," and he informed her that "she was so beautiful that even lions would crouch before her." "She is so vain and flighty that her anger was at once soothed on hearing this." In 1587 the death-warrant of Mary Queen of Scots was signed by her at Richmond. The letters to the Deputy Lieutenants of the maritime counties, announcing the appearance of the Spanish Armada off the coast, were dated from Richmond in the following year. In 1589 she resided there for a considerable time, the air having been prescribed for her health. The prescription appears to have answered, since we are informed in a contemporary letter that "six or seven galliards in a morning, besides music and singing, is her ordinary exercise." In 1602 the French Ambassador was entertained at Richmond, and in the following year the great Queen, worn out by old age and the cares of State, repaired thither to recover, as was hoped, but in truth to die. Her death took place on March 24, 1603, and her successor James VI. of Scotland was immediately proclaimed King of England upon the spot. This was the last memorable incident in the history of Richmond Palace, and the last pageant it saw was the melancholy one of the water procession which bore the body of Elizabeth to interment at Westminster. James preferred Windsor to Richmond; his heir-apparent, however, the idolised Prince Henry, frequently lived there, and was thought to have imbibed the seeds of his fatal illness by imprudent bathing in the Thames. Three years after his death (1615) Prince Charles set up his court there, and formed a valuable collection of pictures. But the place was not a favourite one with him, and after coming to the throne he rarely visited it, though his sons were partly brought up in it. The issue of the Civil War exposed it like other royal palaces to dilapidation at the hands of the victorious Parliament. The Vandalism of this and similar proceedings has affixed a deep stain on the Long Parliament in the opinion of antiquaries and artists. It must be owned, however, that it is not easy to see what other course could have been adopted. Royal palaces, except when adapted for use as public offices, had become a solecism under the new order of things, the edifices were too extensive to be sold or let to private persons, and the idea of palaces for the people, whose artistic treasures should be the general property of the community, was scarcely formed in the seventeenth century. It is nevertheless the fact that the destruction not only of Richmond but of Theobalds, Holmby, and so many other royal residences, and the dismantling of so many castles, memorials of the feudal and mediæval period, to say nothing of the havoc of stained glass and monumental brasses in the churches, impaired the national treasure of picturesqueness as much as the destruction of the monasteries had done in the preceding century. The dispersion of the collection of pictures formed by Charles I. with such judgment and taste, though throwing the cultivation of the national taste back by generations, was probably regarded by all as an inevitable sequel of the abolition of royalty, and at all events saved the nation from the deeper disgrace which would have attended their almost certain conversion into money at the hands of the Merry Monarch. The demolition of the palace by order of the authorities was at all events the means of our obtaining fuller information respecting it than would have existed if it had passed into private hands or been left to decay. From a full survey made by authority of Parliament, which has been preserved, we learn many particulars tending to complete the general impression derived from the views which have been preserved. The name by which the palace was usually known was, we learn, Richmond Court. It was, according to the Commissioners, a two-storied building, built of freestone and roofed with lead. The kitchens and domestic offices seem to have occupied the whole of the lower storey. Chief among these was "one very large room called the Great Buttery." The upper storey contained one "fayr and large room called the Great Hall," the dimensions of which are stated as 100 feet in length and 40 feet in breadth. It had a screen, a gallery, a tiled floor, and eleven ornamental statues; it is stated to have been very well lighted and ceiled; and yet, perhaps from the difficulty of warming so large an apartment, it does not appear to have had a fireplace. In lieu of this was "in the midst a brick hearth for a charcoal fire, having a large lanthorn in the roof of the hall fitted for that purpose." The smoke must surely have created very considerable inconvenience, and the peculiarity, which would have scandalised no one in Henry VII.'s time, may perhaps account for the comparative disuse of Richmond by royalty as the requirements of civilisation became more exacting. The Commissioners confirm the accuracy of the views by further speaking of a third storey; it would appear that some part of the structure must have been raised. Twelve rooms, "most of them matted," are spoken of as existing on this storey. They were probably bed-chambers, several of which are stated to be extant without any specification of the exact locality. The Duke of York's (the future James II.'s) bed-chamber and school-chamber are mentioned, as are also apartments for pages. The dimensions of the chapel are given as 96 feet by 30, "with handsome cathedral seats and pews, a removable pulpit, and a fayre case of carved work for a pair of organs." There is also a detailed account of the Wardrobe Buildings, the only portion of the Palace of which any vestiges remain— interesting for the enumeration of the various officers of the court quartered therein—"the cup-bearer, carver, server, grooms of the privy chamber, the spicery, chandelry, cofferer, the clerk of green cloth, apothecary, confectioner, housekeeper, wardrobe and wardrobe keeper, porter, chaplains, and gentlemen of the bed-chamber." The particulars of the offices are very minute, and suggest many curious points of note and query. Mention is made of "one very large fountain of lead," which is believed to be the same as that now at St. Ervans, Lord Windsor's seat in Glamorganshire. In describing the turrets which make so conspicuous a figure in the view, the Commissioners become almost poetical: "Fourteen turretts, which very much adorn and set forth the fabric of the whole structure, and are a very graceful ornament unto the whole house, being perspicuous to the country round about." "Richmond Green," it is added, "contains twenty acres more or less excellent land, to be depastured only with sheep; it is well turfed, level, and a special ornament to the Palace." It was planted with 113 elm trees.

The value placed by the Commissioners upon the materials of Richmond Court was £10,782 : 10 : 2, and it was sold for £10,000 to Thomas

Rookesby, William Goodwin, and Adam Baynes, from whom it subsequently passed to Sir Gregory Norton, one of the judges of Charles I., from whom it was reclaimed at the Restoration. According to Fuller, it had been entirely razed, but this must be an exaggeration, for it was granted as a residence to the Queen Dowager, Henrietta Maria, and she actually lived there till 1665. It may, however, well be believed to have been "in an almost ruinous condition." After her departure to France she made over her interest in the manor to Sir Edward Villiers. A relative, Lady Frances Villiers, was governess to the Duke of York's children, who were established here under her charge, but both his sons

The Palace of Richmond. From an Engraving by Buck, 1737.

died in 1667. At a later date Sir Edward Villiers resigned the manor to the duke, then or shortly afterwards James II. James's son, the forlorn young Pretender, is said to have been brought up here for a time, but, if so, the period must have been very brief indeed. Queen Anne wished to have the place as a site for the erection of a residence, but, failing from the opposition of the lessee, appears to have let the remainder as far as possible. The last reference to the Palace as in any manner existing is the mention of it by Strype in 1720 as "now decayed and parcelled out in tenements."

> The gentle *Thames*
> And the green silent pastures yet remain.

It will be convenient to add to the history of Richmond Palace a short account of the more important of the various religious establishments which formerly existed at Richmond, as they are both royal and mediæval foundations. The most considerable were the Priory of Shene, the Nunnery of St. Bridget, on the site where Syon House stands at present, and the Friary.

The Priory and the Nunnery owed their existence to the conscientious scruples of Henry V., who, within a year of his coming to the throne, founded both to expiate the guilt which his father Henry IV. had contracted by the dethronement and murder of his predecessor. The Priory was erected for forty monks of the Carthusian Order, under the name of "The House of Jesus of Bethlehem at Sheen." According to Aubrey, the dimensions were very considerable, the great hall being no less than 132 feet in length by 24 in width; and the great quadrangle 360 feet by 100; with cloisters 600 feet long. The endowment corresponded to the magnificence of the structure, and comprised the proceeds of Shene and Petersham weirs, as well as the privilege of annually importing four pipes of Gascony wine. The principal events in its history are the sanctuary it afforded to Perkin Warbeck, who was only given up upon condition that his life should be spared; and, if a very doubtful story be authentic, the deposition in it of the body of the Scottish king James IV. after his death at Flodden. It was suppressed in 1539, and although restored for a short time under Mary, was again abandoned at the accession of Elizabeth. The monks are said to have retired to Flanders. The Priory Church is stated by the Parliamentary Commissioners to be in a ruinous condition; it must, however, have for some time survived the dissolution of the monastery, if it be the fact that Leicester was here married to Amy Robsart in the presence of King Edward VI. After several changes of ownership, it became the property of Sir William Temple, to whose residence on the spot we shall recur.

Syon Nunnery was founded by Henry at the same time as Shene Priory, for sixty nuns of the Order of St. Bridget, and enjoyed the same privileges as the other foundation. The king's purpose is said to have been that devotion should be absolutely unintermittent, one commencing as the other left off; but this would be hard to reconcile with monastic rule, and is probably a mere legend growing out of the proximity of the two convents. There is no doubt, however, that Henry was a religious prince, and deeply sensible of the imperfection of his title, and his foundation of the convents at a place in which he so delighted is a proof of the interest which he took in them. Syon Nunnery also was suppressed by Henry VIII., who reserved the gardens for his own use.

The third principal religious establishment, commonly called "The Friary," was of later date than the others, having been founded by

Remains of the Palace, Richmond. Drawn by Clough Bromley.

Henry VII. about 1499 as a convent of Observant Friars. If a view given by the historians of Richmond is authentic, it was a handsome edifice, in close proximity to the Palace, with a fine church and extensive cloisters. It shared the general fate of religious houses at the dissolution of the monasteries.

CHAPTER II

RICHMOND UNDER THE HOUSE OF HANOVER—DISTINGUISHED RESIDENTS

UP to the period of the abandonment and virtual destruction of the old palace, the history of Richmond is chiefly connected with royalty. The age of suburban villas, unconnected with the possession of landed property, was not yet. Country gentlemen generally possessed domains upon which their duties and their interests alike obliged them to reside, and their usual dwellings were castles and manor-houses. The overwhelming proportions of the royal residence, moreover, as we now see in Windsor, did not encourage the growth of minor residences under its shadow; while it may be not unfairly conjectured that the aggregation under the royal roof of men-at-arms, cooks, scullions, grooms, and serving-men of all denominations, so graphically described by the Spanish visitor in Queen Mary's time, must have operated as a considerable discouragement. Wolsey, as we have seen, found it convenient to be at least as far off as Hampton; perhaps if he had gone further still he would not have found it necessary to sacrifice his palace to appease his master's jealousy. The relinquishment of Richmond as a royal residence coincides pretty exactly with the development of wealth, taste, and the love of ease which conduces to the occupation of rural abodes in delightful situations, not generally as the occupant's sole habitation, but as an appendage to the dwelling where the serious business of his life is carried on, or perhaps as a retreat for his old age. In a word, about the middle of the seventeenth century Richmond passes from the estate of palacedom to that of villadom. Not that its connection with royalty is closed—we shall still have much to relate respecting the earlier princes of the House of Hanover—but even the royal residence is more of a villa than a palace, and it becomes more and more of a retreat for private persons of distinction, whose varied characters contribute the more picturesque features to its history. One circumstance, which greatly favoured the transformation of Richmond, was the extent of ground gained by the appropriation, not only of the ancient palace and monasteries, but of the "ample enclosures" which had begirt them, and which it was both convenient and profitable to occupy with handsome buildings. Evelyn records in his diary, August 27, 1678, "I dined at Mr. Henry Brouncker's, at the Abbey of Sheene, formerly a monastery of Carthusians, there yet remaining one of their solitary cells, with a cross. Within this ample enclosure are several pretty villas and fine gardens of the most excellent fruits, especially Sir William Temple's, and Lord Lisle, son to the Earl of Leicester, who has divers rare pictures there, above all that of Sir Brian Tuke by Holbein." Richmond was clearly passing from the monarchical into the aristocratical period of its history. Charles II., indeed, bestowed the name of the town as a ducal title upon one of his natural children, by whose descendants it is still borne. But his favourite resort for recreation was Newmarket, and when he planned the erection of a new palace, the site was to have been at Winchester. When, in 1669, the Grand Duke of Tuscany travelled in England, he duly visited Hampton Court, which he caused to be depicted by an artist in his train, and the beautiful drawing may be seen in the English translation of the elaborate account of his travels drawn up by Magalotti, one of his retinue. Magalotti, however, though sufficiently circumstantial as regards Hampton, says not a word about Richmond. Pepys names it only thrice, and all his references are insignificant.

Sir William Temple is undoubtedly one of the persons whose residence at Richmond has contributed to bestow intellectual distinction upon the town. He had, as already mentioned, become possessed of the lease of the suppressed Priory at Shene, and his residence dates from the year 1666. Among the numerous elegant tastes of this highly accomplished man, the most engrossing was that for the cultivation of fruit and flowers, for which, indeed, the age of Charles II. was especially distinguished. "My heart," he writes in 1667, "is set on my little corner at Sheen, that while I keep it no other disappointments will be sensible to me. I am contriving this summer how a succession of cherries may be compassed from May to Michaelmas, and how the riches of Sheen vines may be improved by half-a-dozen sorts, which are not known here." In another letter he speaks of laying out a thousand pounds upon his garden. Evelyn writes on March 24, 1688: "After dinner we went to see Sir William Temple's. The most remarkable things are his orangery and gardens, where the wall fruit trees are most exquisitely nailed and trained, far better than I ever noted." Temple had at this date resided regularly at Shene for eight years, having settled entirely there after his renunciation of political life in 1680. His abode there led to the only important association of Richmond with William III., who sometimes visited Temple to seek his advice upon political matters, and some of these visits may have been paid while Temple lived at Shene. More were perhaps paid to Moor Park, not far from Godalming, whither Temple retired under deep dejection from the death of his son, preferring it, it is said, on account of its greater distance from London. There he created another earthly paradise, according to the notions of his day. "The grounds," says Macaulay, "were laid out with the angular regularity which Sir William had admired in the flower-beds of Haarlem and the Hague. A beautiful rivulet, flowing from the hills of Surrey, bounded the domain. But a straight canal which, bordered by a terrace, intersected the garden, was probably more admired by the lovers of the picturesque in that age." There it was that the king met the "eccentric, uncouth, disagreeable young Irishman, who attended Sir William as an amanuensis for board and twenty pounds a year," whose name was Jonathan Swift, and whom he instructed in cutting asparagus after the Dutch fashion.

But little is heard of the town of Richmond under Queen Anne, except for the splendour of the mansion built or restored by the Duke of Ormond, after whose exile it passed to his brother, the Earl of Arran, who in 1721 sold it to the Prince of Wales, afterwards George II. The Princess Caroline, afterwards Queen, conceived a great attachment to the place, and so it came to pass that the Prince was residing there when the news of his father's death arrived in England, and the scene took place described with such incomparable vividness, though not with extraordinary accuracy, in Thackeray's *Four Georges*.

"In the afternoon of June 14, 1727, two horsemen might have been perceived galloping along the road from Chelsea to Richmond. The foremost, cased in the jack-boots of the period, was a broad-faced, jolly-looking, and very corpulent cavalier; but, by the manner in which he urged his horse, you might see that he was a bold as well as a skilful rider. He speedily reached Richmond Lodge, and asked to see the owner of the mansion. The mistress of the house and her ladies, to whom our friend was admitted, said he could not be introduced to the master, however pressing the business might be. The master was asleep after his dinner; he always slept after his dinner; and woe be to the person who interrupted him! Nevertheless, our stout friend of the jack-boots put the affrighted ladies aside, opened the forbidden door of the bedroom, where upon the bed lay a little gentleman; and here the eager messenger lay down in his jack-boots.

"He on the bed started up, and with many oaths and a strong German accent asked who was there, and who dared to disturb him.

"'I am Sir Robert Walpole,' said the messenger. The awakened sleeper hated Sir Robert Walpole. 'I have the honour to announce to your Majesty that your royal father, King George I., died at Osnaburg on Saturday last.'

"'*Dat is one big lie!*' roared out his sacred Majesty."

This lively account is not entirely in accordance with fact. Lord Hervey, Sir Robert Walpole's staunch adherent, who is certain to have been correctly informed, tells us that when Sir Robert arrived the Princess was with the Prince in his chamber, that he was immediately announced by the Duchess of Dorset and admitted without delay, and that all he said was, "I am come to acquaint your Majesty with the death of your father." Nor did the king, although "extremely surprised," utter the uncomplimentary ejaculation which Thackeray has placed in his mouth, though what he did say must have been even less acceptable to Walpole's ears, "Go to Chiswick and take your directions from Sir Spencer Compton." History records how the king's benevolent intentions towards Sir Spencer were reconsidered upon the discovery that Walpole was far better qualified to manage

Richmond Lodge. *From a Water-colour Drawing in the Crace Collection, British Museum.*

his affairs, *i.e.* to extract money for the Civil List out of the country; and that it was to this, and by no means to the comparatively insignificant qualification of being the wisest and ablest statesman of his day, that he owed the continuance of his premiership. The history has always excited indignation and ridicule; in fact, however, there is more to be said for George II. than appears at first sight. The great contests of the preceding century were being fought over again on a petty and contracted arena. Charles I. had been guilty of falsehood and perfidy, not from natural inclination, or even weakness of character, but because he honestly believed such weapons allowable in conflict with rebels and traitors, in which light he regarded all who endeavoured to limit his prerogative. George II. and his queen, with their German education, were quite as firmly persuaded that the revenue of the country was by right the private property of the sovereign, and naturally gauged the merits of a Prime Minister by his ability to help them to their own.

So able was Walpole's management, that Parliament bestowed upon the queen both Richmond Lodge and Somerset House, together with £100,000 a year, "just double," says Lord Hervey, "what any Queen of England had ever had before." Upon the queen's fatal illness, ten years afterwards, the king was so anxious to learn whether, by the terms of the jointure, Richmond Lodge would pass to his abhorred son, that he sent Lord Hervey to fetch the Chancellor off the bench, and ascertain his opinion. It appeared that the king had a life-interest, and death interfered to prevent the prince inheriting. We are indebted to Lord Hervey's mordant pen for some curious glimpses both of the Lodge at this time and of its royal occupants. "The king and queen," he says, "were always so much in private at Richmond (and indeed the house would not allow them to be much in public), that they saw nobody but their servants." The "prospect of the royal palace," as engraved, does indeed indicate a secluded, walled-in spot, but it would also seem as though the public were in some degree admitted to the garden. At a later period (1752) the grounds were open during the summer by order of the king, whose respect for public rights, to his honour be it recorded, was so great that he refused to take steps to abate the nuisance of a brick-kiln in troublesome proximity to the palace. In another place Lord Hervey speaks of the thinness of the partitions, which allowed a conversation between the king and Lady Suffolk to be overheard. After the session of 1727, "the king went to Richmond, as he said, because it was an old acquaintance; he went afterwards to Hampton Court and Windsor, as others said, because they were new acquaintances." [He had never been on visiting terms with his father.] "He would fain have persuaded both himself and other people that he loved leisure and retirement; but whenever he tried them he was always uneasy and impatient to return to a circle, and never did retire in order to convince people he liked it, without convincing himself that he did not, and that he was no more turned to live alone agreeably to himself than he was to live in company agreeably to other people." This passage is a good example of the love of pointed antithesis and *manie de briller*, which characterises the style of this most Gallicised of all our eminent authors, and frequently renders him untrustworthy by mere force of manner, when the substance would have passed without comment in the hands of a dull writer.

The connection of Frederick Prince of Wales with Richmond will be best described in conjunction with Kew, where he resided. The extremely bad terms on which he lived with his royal parents rarely allowed him to show himself at Richmond Lodge, which was the special delight of Queen Caroline, "at whose expense," says an inscription on a contemporary plan, "it is made complete, being augmented with buildings and sundry large parcels of ground purchased to enlarge the garden, park, etc., all curiously, and at no small expense, adorned in so exquisite a manner as renders it second to none in the kingdom." The queen's decorations were in some respects more creditable to her enthusiasm than to her taste. Everybody, it has been wisely said, should have one horse and one hobby, and the hobby of this sensible and practical woman was her "Merlin's Cave," something between a grotto and a waxwork. Externally, the cave was thatched, and if not awe-inspiring, was certainly uninviting, internally. An engraving reproduced in Mr. Chancellor's *History of Richmond* represents a portentous scene of waxen magicians and knights standing in niches, pre-eminent among them Merlin, who is delivering his wondrous glass globe to King Ryence. The theme and the accompanying verses are derived from Spenser, and the

one satisfactory feature of the whole is the apparent testimony that
The Faery Queene was read at Court in the most prosaic age of
English literature. Otherwise, while lamenting the king's rudeness, we
cannot widely dissent from the spirit of the remark which Lord Hervey
records him to have made to the queen, when she observed that Merlin's
cave had been abused in the opposition newspaper, *The Craftsman*. "I
am very glad of it; you deserve to be abused for such childish, silly stuff,
and it is the first time I ever knew the scoundrel to be in the right."
His Majesty would have been still more emphatic if he had known that
he was himself paying for the stuff in question. "The king believed,"
says Horace Walpole, "she paid for all with her own money, nor would
he even look at her intended plans, saying he did not care how she flung
away her own revenue. He little suspected the aids Sir Robert furnished
her from the treasury. When she died, she was indebted £20,000 to
the king." This sum, of course, had been by no means exclusively
expended upon Merlin's cave. The queen also kept up the gardens in
magnificent style; had a more intellectual toy than the cave in "The
Hermitage," a little garden retreat where she asserted the character
she really deserved as a patroness of philosophy and science, by
adorning the rooms with busts of Newton, Locke, and other illustrious
personages, and forming a library. She also hung the walls with
drawings erroneously believed to be by Holbein, which she had herself
discovered in a bureau at Kensington Palace, and which were probably
part of the collection now at Windsor Castle. Her librarian was
Stephen Duck, a thatcher, whose accomplishment of verse caused
him to be regarded as a prodigy, and who was, at all events, no
worse a poet than the Laureate, Colley Cibber. The queen, who as
princess had behaved munificently to Milton's daughter, had Stephen
educated for the Church, and assisted him with her patronage. It
could not have escaped Her Majesty's attention that all the eminent
literary men of the day, with unprecedented unanimity, were in
opposition; but the balance was not likely to be redressed by
Stephen Duck, who, years after the queen's death, became hypo-
chondriacal and committed suicide. All Queen Caroline's creations,
and Richmond Lodge itself, vanished about 1770, when George III.,
who in the early years of his reign had frequently resided there,

destroyed the whole, and converted the estate into a pasturage for cattle. Brown, the royal gardener, was supposed to have brought this about, as Mason sings :—

> Come then, prolific art, and with thee bring
> The charms that rise from thy exhaustless spring ;
> To Richmond come, for, see, untutored Brown
> Destroys those wonders that were once thy own.
> Lo ! from his melon ground the peasant slave
> Has rudely rushed and levelled Merlin's cave,
> Knocked down the waxen wizard, seized his wand,
> Transformed to lawns what late was fairyland ;
> And marred with impious hand each sweet design
> Of Stephen Duck and good Queen Caroline.

One probably unauthentic passage in the history of Richmond Lodge under George II. has, it is needless to say, obtained immortality in literature—the journey and petition of Jeanie Deans to Queen Caroline told in Scott's *Heart of Midlothian*, although he erroneously places the lodge in the park ; and there is no evidence of Helen Walker, the real prototype of the imaginary Jeanie, having ever visited Richmond, or having had an interview with the queen, although she undoubtedly saw the Duke of Argyle. A lively account of the feelings of the Court with reference to the Porteous riots may be found in Lord Hervey's *Memoirs*, and fully justifies Scott's picture of the attitude assumed in the first instance by the queen towards the duke.

In the reign of George II. Richmond was rendered illustrious by the residence of the most distinguished poet who ever made it his permanent abode, but it does not seem to be precisely known when James Thomson first became one of its inhabitants, and whether the line inscribed on his house—

> Here Thomson sang the seasons, and their change—

is accurate in any respect. "Winter," the first published of his cantos on the Seasons, was written in Scotland before he came to England. He was undoubtedly an inhabitant of the metropolis for some time after its publication in 1726, and the entire work was completed by 1730. His later works were no doubt composed at Richmond, among them the only one which, besides *The Seasons*, gives him a title to rank high as a poet, *The Castle of Indolence*. This theme was exceedingly well adapted

Thomson's Summer-house. From an Engraving by W. B. Cooke, after G. Barnard.

to his genius, if it is true that he might be seen in his garden on a summer afternoon with his hands in his pockets, browsing off the tree upon the peaches which he was too lazy to gather. The anecdote is corroborated by all we know of him, especially by the reminiscences of his gossiping barber, preserved in the *Mirror* for 1823, which convey a lively picture of the lazy, corpulent, somewhat bibulous, but amiable and honourable bard, who, after all, overcame his natural sloth so far as to produce a great deal of verse of the quality which Coleridge, a kindred spirit in not a few respects, thought had on the whole better *not* be produced.

> Building up the rhyme
> When he had better far have stretched his limbs
> Beside a brook in sunny forest dell,
> By sun or moonlight ; to the influences
> Of shapes and sounds and shifting elements
> Surrendering his whole spirit, of his song
> And of his fame forgetful ! so his fame
> Should share in Nature's immortality,
> A venerable thing ! and so his song
> Should make all Nature lovelier, and itself
> Be loved like Nature.

We give, from a drawing by Barnard, a view of the summer-house where *The Seasons* were written, or supposed to have been written, beneath its umbrageous tree.

Thomson's house is supposed to be preserved, but would appear to be in the condition of the Irishman's gun with its new stock, new lock, and new barrel. Lord Buchan perpetuated his local memory by a brass tablet in the parish church, but for which the spot where his remains are deposited would have been forgotten ; for although the local historians conjecture that his epitaph has been covered up by pews, Dr. Johnson expressly informs us that there never was any, his memory having been deemed sufficiently honoured by a cenotaph in Westminster Abbey. The cause of his death is generally stated to have been cold taken on the river, but the barber asserts it to have been imprudent conviviality in the society of the actor Quin, aggravated by improper medicine. Quin, the most eminent actor of his day after Garrick, is also to be enumerated among distinguished Richmond residents. He must have been a terrible personage in the eyes of the reminiscent barber, who records of him : " One day he asked particularly if the razor was in good order, and protested that he had as many barbers' ears in his parlour at home as any boy had birds' eggs on a string; and swore that if I did not shave him smoothly he would add mine to the number."

Thomson's memory called forth the well-known lines of Collins, too long, and disfigured by the absurd appellation of Druid bestowed on the dead poet, but distinguished nevertheless by a simplicity and nature unusual at the period. They certainly suggested, though probably quite unconsciously, to Wordsworth his memorable "Poet's Epitaph," and avowedly inspired the first lyrical verses he wrote, or at least published.

Richmond Church. Drawn by Clough Bromley.

These were composed at the age of nineteen, and being less known, may be cited here:—

> Glide gently, thus for ever glide,
> O Thames! that other bards may see
> As lovely visions by thy side
> As now, fair river, come to me.
> O glide, fair stream! for ever so,
> Thy quiet soul on all bestowing,
> Till all our minds for ever flow
> As thy deep waters now are flowing.
>
> Vain thought!—Yet be as now thou art,
> That in thy waters may be seen
> The image of a poet's heart,
> How bright, how solemn, how serene!
> Such as did once the Poet bless,
> Who murmuring here a later ditty,

Could find no refuge from distress
But in the milder grief of pity.

Now let us, as we float along,
For *him* suspend the dashing oar,
And pray that never child of song
May know that Poet's sorrows more.
How calm! how still! the only sound,
The dripping of the oar suspended!
—The evening darkness gathers round,
By virtue's holiest Powers attended.

*Sir Joshua Reynolds' House on Richmond Hill. By J. Farrington, R.A.
Engraved by T. Huson, R.P.E.*

The next important private resident at Richmond is Sir Joshua Reynolds, and one more distinguished could hardly be found, but no reminiscence of him connected with the place seems to be recorded, except his having once met the king on a walk, and received His Majesty's congratulations on his election as Mayor of Plympton in Devonshire. His house, now called Wick House, was built for him by Sir William Chambers, but, although erected by the first architect of the day for the first painter, was singularly unadorned and unattractive. It is still standing, but the original brick has been entirely encased in stucco.

The local historians are certain that Sir Joshua must necessarily have brought down wits, poets, and painters from London, and very probably he did, but no record of their proceedings remains. It is indeed probable that his sojourns at Richmond mostly took place when town was empty, for a portrait painter of his eminence could not have afforded to be out of the way of his sitters during the London season. We give a reproduction of his curiously idealised but beautiful " View from Richmond

*The View from Richmond Hill. By Sir Joshua Reynolds.
Engraved by T. Huson, R.P.E.*

Hill." It is just such as an Italian artist might have painted at home from recollection of the scene.

Another important inhabitant of Richmond, whose connection with the place probably commenced during the time of Reynolds, was indeed a man of a different class. The Duke of Queensberry exemplifies the truth of Goethe's saying, that the final judgment of the world on any person depends greatly upon the character in which he last presents himself to its observation. In the popular estimate Queensberry is the " Old Q." of the first decade of the nineteenth century, familiar to London loungers as he sat in his balcony in Piccadilly, ogling pretty passers-by with the only eye available for this purpose, and, as was generally believed, with a saddled horse and a messenger in readiness to pursue any woman or any horse so fortunate as to attract his Grace's especial notice. It is surprising to be assured that in the opinion of those who knew him best the duke surpassed most men in shrewd common-sense; and his correspondence with George Selwyn exhibits him in the light of a kind, staunch, and self-sacrificing friend. The key to the infirmities of his character seems to be that, like Charles II., he had an excess of common-sense unassociated with any ideal or patriotic aspiration which would have pointed out a befitting employment of his vast wealth and remarkable abilities. The consequent course of selfish dissipation, relieved only by charities which, although munificent, imposed no trouble upon the benefactor, gradually wore down an originally buoyant nature until the spirited youth became the sated voluptuary, one of whose sayings is almost the most impressive warning on record of the Nemesis which awaits those who live solely for pleasure. "The dinner," Wilberforce records of an occasion when he enjoyed the duke's hospitality, "was sumptuous, the views from the villa quite enchanting, and the Thames in all its glory; but the duke looked on with indifference. 'What is there,' he said, 'to make so much of in the Thames? I am quite weary of it; there it goes, flow, flow, flow, always the same.'"

The villa where this tragic confession of mental decrepitude was uttered had been built in 1708 by the Earl of Cholmondeley on the site of the old Palace, and greatly improved by the Duke of Queensberry, who filled it with choice statues and paintings, and one of the finest collections of shells then extant. Among its curiosities was said to be the identical tapestry which had decorated the Court of Chancery during Clarendon's chancellorship. It was abandoned by the duke about the end of the eighteenth century out of resentment for a lawsuit instituted against him by the inhabitants of Richmond for an illegal enclosure of public land. The townsmen were quite right in protecting their property, even at the risk of alienating a wealthy benefactor, but the duke seems to have been unconscious of offence, and perhaps a little diplomacy might not have been out of place. At his death he bequeathed it to Maria Fagniani, a young lady of ambiguous paternity, whom the duke,

The Thames and Richmond Hill, from the Earl of Cholmondeley's House, 1749.

who had no legitimate issue, chose to consider in the light of a daughter. Lord Yarmouth complaisantly made her his wife, and was rewarded by a residuary legateeship under the duke's will equivalent to £200,000. Maria thus ultimately became Marchioness of Hertford, but for excellent reasons always resided in Paris, and the unoccupied mansion was pulled down in 1829.

Very different associations are connected with the names of Horace Walpole's friends, the fascinating and accomplished Misses Berry, who did so much to brighten the last years of the veteran wit and virtuoso. His first acquaintance with them was made in 1787; they soon became indispensable to him, and never strayed far from the spot where they had known him. When, at length, in 1852, they were laid to rest in Petersham Churchyard, their epitaph, written by the Earl of Carlisle, could say that they reposed "amidst scenes which in life they had frequented and loved, followed by the tender regret of those who close the unbroken succession of friends devoted to them with fond affection during every step of their long career." "Few women at eighty-two," the elder Miss Berry had written in 1845, "have so little to complain of." Another aged lady connected alike with Richmond and with the literary history of the eighteenth century was Miss Mary Langton, daughter of Johnson's friend Bennet Langton and his own godchild, to whom, in her seventh year, he being himself in the last year of his life, he addressed the pretty letter preserved by Boswell, commencing, "My dearest Miss Jenny." When, nearly seventy years afterwards, Mr. Crisp, the historian of Richmond, called upon Miss Langton by her invitation, he found her surrounded by Johnsonian relics, the letter, above all things, framed and glazed, "the cup and saucer out of which he last drank his favourite beverage, the chair on which he usually sat, the table at which he generally wrote, a few of the pictures which had originally ornamented the walls of his dwelling." Where are they now? Yet another interesting female inhabitant of Richmond may be mentioned in the person of Barbara Hofland, who died here in November 1844. Mrs. Hofland's name is still preserved by her affecting story, *The Son of a Genius;* and her reputation would stand high if she had refused to defer to what now seems the intolerably artificial and stilted style prescribed by the taste of her day for juvenile fiction. Such was not her own preference; her letters to Miss Mitford are among the best published in the latter's voluminous correspondence, and reveal her as the possessor of a bright and lively talent. Her husband, the landscape painter T. C. Hofland, is remembered as the author of one of the most agreeable books on angling in the language, and is especially associated with Richmond as the painter of one of the best views of Richmond

Richmond Theatre. From an old Engraving. Reproduced by T. Huson, R.P.E.

Hill, which has unfortunately proved incapable of reproduction for the illustration of this monograph.

Among the more distinguished residents at Richmond in the present century must be named Edmund Kean, whose stormy career, comparable to the description given of his own performance of *Macbeth*, that it was like seeing Shakespeare by flashes of lightning, terminated here in 1833. For a considerable period during his later years he conducted the Richmond theatre, where he had frequently acted in his palmy days. At this period he appeared when off the stage but a shadow of his old self, and excited the compassion of those who saw him creeping about supported by his celebrated agate-handled stick; but in the evening, Antæus-like, he regained his strength as he trod the familiar boards, and his Othello and Sir Giles Overreach were still instinct with passion and power. At Richmond, too, Kean was buried, followed to the grave by almost all the representatives of the dramatic profession in London. Lady Martin made her *début* at the little Richmond theatre, and it had several flashes of success before its final disappearance in 1884. Our illustration shows its homely and almost rural appearance at the beginning of this century. It was built about 1760. It had been preceded by theatres opened by Penkethman in 1749 and by T. Cibber. The latter sought to evade the penalties against unlicensed entertainments under colour of an establishment for the sale of "cephalic snuff." An earlier place of amusement had been popular from the beginning of the century under the name of "Richmond Wells," which arose out of the discovery of a medicinal spring in 1689, and was at one time very popular, but having become the resort of low characters, was extinguished as a nuisance about 1780.

The last illustrious resident at Richmond to be mentioned is a great foreign statesman, who, like so many of his kind, put into England in stress of politics. Metternich's connection with Richmond was not intimate, and we name it chiefly for the sake of quoting the letter of Disraeli's, in which it is mentioned, and which shows that he also had thought of Richmond as a possible retreat :—

May 2, 1849.

I have been to see Metternich. He lives on Richmond Green, in the most charming house in the world, called the Old Palace—long library, gardens, everything worthy of him. I met there the Duchess of Cambridge and the Colloredos. I am enchanted with Richmond Green, which, strange to say, I don't recollect ever having visited before, often as I have been to Richmond. I should like to let my house and live there. It is still and sweet, charming alike in summer and winter.

CHAPTER III

THE PARK—THE HILL—THE RIVER

It affords some presumption that Richmond Palace, from the time of Edward I. until long afterwards, was not regarded as a royal residence of the first class, that so little mention is made of the existence of any royal park, chase, or warren in connection with it. It cannot be conceived that any Plantagenet king ever passed any considerable time without hunting, and opportunities for the enjoyment of sport cannot have been wholly wanting; for when, in 1528, the French Ambassador was lodged at Richmond, he had permission to hunt in every one of the king's parks there. Yet there was certainly no very extensive domain at hand, and the inference seems to be that Richmond was looked upon rather as a retreat for occasional recreation than as a regular residence. In the earliest views we possess, the Palace appears as though plumped down on the bare ground, and devoid of any park, garden, or ornamental appendage of any kind, but this can only bespeak the rudeness of the artist. In an old view of the Palace, said to be taken from an ancient picture, deer are represented as being chased in an enclosure immediately contiguous to the Palace itself, but this probably proceeded from the artist's desire to embellish his work, or to depict Richmond as both palace and hunting-seat on the same principle which sometimes led the early painters to represent several actions of the same person upon a single canvas. The anonymous writer, at least, to whom we have already been obliged for a description of the Old Palace when it was a creation of yesterday, mentions an entertainment given by Henry to Spanish envoys, probably in 1502, from which it appears that the green immediately fronting the Palace was used for shooting at targets,

The Thames from the Buccleugh Gardens, Richmond.

and that after witnessing the performance of the yeomen of the guard, the party repaired to the park, "where the king caused wanlaces to be made and the deer to be brought about. And there the Earl of Hispayne strake a deer with his cross-bow, and great slaughter was of venison by the said estraungers and brought into the quarry." According to Mr. Jesse, this old park "appears to have been situated on the northeast of Richmond, between what are now called the royal gardens and the river." The new Park was the acquisition of Charles I. Prior to about 1634 it was an extensive tract, partly waste, known as Shene Chase, over a portion of which the king himself possessed rights. The remainder "consisted of a number of small farms and houses in private tenure, having extensive grounds attached to them, with commons and waste lands belonging to the various parishes." It seems somewhat unaccountable that Charles, who in general showed so little partiality to Richmond, should have taken it into his head to enclose this particular tract as a royal hunting-ground, which would be of little service to him unless he were prepared to reside frequently on the spot. Not only, however, did he form the design, but, erecting without further ceremony a wall which "made those who were unwilling to part with their estates more flexible," he adhered to it with such tenacity that Laud, Juxon, and Lord Treasurer Cottington among them were unable to dissuade him from a project manifestly impolitic at so troublesome a time, and which Clarendon enumerates among the causes of the Civil War. By his obstinacy in carrying it out, Charles became in the long-run one of the greatest benefactors Richmond has ever known, but there can be no doubt that its execution was attended with great injustice from the violent confiscation of common rights, and the destruction of farms and private residences, for which the £4000 paid were probably a very inadequate compensation. The commoners appear to have received none whatever. As late as 1662 the daughters of Lord Dysart are found petitioning on this account. The following entry in the *Calendar of State Papers*, January 25, 1637, is exceedingly significant: "Petition from the inhabitants of Mortlake, who desire to be relieved from the ship-money assessment in regard his Majesty has taken into his park at Richmond one half their lands." The case is met by ordering the Sheriff to make an abatement, and lay the sum upon some other part of the county. The opposition of the owners and commoners was, however, at last quieted; labourers were enlisted by an order dated March 28, 1636, and on June 15, 1637, the Earl of Portland was appointed the first ranger. The old rights-of-way were allowed to continue, and gates and step-ladders were provided to facilitate their exercise, a step which no doubt contributed to disarm opposition. We hear nothing of any planting or embellishment, or even of any stocking with deer, though this can hardly have been omitted. "It was a bog and a harbour for deer-stealers and vagabonds," says Horace Walpole, speaking of its condition at the accession of George II. Charles can hardly have made any use of it himself; the year of the enclosure was also that of the commencement of civil strife by the resistance of the Scotch to his attempt to force the English Liturgy upon them. After Charles's death the Parliament, to its honour, did not endeavour to turn the domain into money, but presented it to the City of London, one of the most truly enlightened acts recorded in the history of the seventeenth century. Unfortunately, it cannot be affirmed that the City turned it to any account for the public good, although its venison no doubt found its way to many a City feast. No sooner was the Restoration a certainty, than, ere Charles had landed, the City hastened to restore it to him, asseverating that it had been accepted for no other purpose, an assertion to which the Merry Monarch, among whose faults credulity is not enumerated, doubtless accorded exactly as much credit as it deserved.

Charles II. has little personal connection with the history of Richmond, although shortly after his accession we hear in the State papers of £300 being paid for feeding the deer brought to the Park "for the king's disport," which probably necessitated the considerable expenses also incurred for building and repairing the Park wall. In 1668 it was ordered that the earth required for making bricks for this purpose should be dug in the Park itself, and furze and underwood cut down for burning them. The only anecdote which brings Charles into contact with the Park is that of his having on one occasion made it a blind by pretending a hunting party when the real business was to meet and appease Lady Castlemaine. No other circumstance relating to the Park under him and his immediate successors seems to be preserved, except the names of the rangers. The improvement and beauty of the Park date from the accession of George II., who in October 1727 bestowed the rangership nominally upon Robert, afterwards Earl of Orford, eldest son of Sir Robert Walpole, but virtually upon Walpole himself. The minister, a Norfolk country gentleman, who delighted in a country life and rural sports, carried out great improvements by draining and building at enormous cost the Great Lodge, pulled down

Richmond Park Gate. By J. Brown, 1805.

about half a century ago. While in town he was accustomed to come down for Saturday and Sunday, to repose himself, as he said, but in fact, as was thought, to work with less interruption. The king, however, would occasionally break in upon his retirement, for hunting, according to one account, according to another for shooting, and, if Horace Walpole's word may be taken, by no means objected to libations of punch. If shooting was His Majesty's object, the game may very probably have been the American wild turkeys, of which large flocks were kept in the Park about this period. They were eventually destroyed for the same reason as that which White in his *Natural History of Selborne* tells us induced Bishop Hoadley to give up keeping deer, the sanguinary affrays which they occasioned between poachers and gamekeepers. Another interesting race of feathered inhabitants, the herons, have alternately flourished and decayed at various periods, and their fate appears to be at present trembling in the balance.

Walpole as virtual ranger did one thing which he had no right to do, and which, after his time, gave occasion to one of the most picturesque passages in the history of Richmond. He violated the understanding which had subsisted between the Crown and the public since the formation of the Park by Charles I. He took away the step-ladders which gave access over the walls, and only allowed entrance through the gates, and this by ticket. The tickets were probably at first issued with liberality; at all events, no objection is recorded during the rangership of Lord Orford, who died in 1751. Upon his death, however, the office was conferred upon the Princess Amelia, who from the first adopted an illiberal course, and before long entirely closed the Park to the neighbourhood, granting a few tickets only to favoured individuals. Private remonstrances and appeals through the press proving fruitless, the inhabitants of Richmond, encouraged, it is said, by the Duke of Newcastle, who certainly did not love the Princess Amelia, commenced a suit for the restoration of their rights. The nominal plaintiff was a patriotic townsman, John Lewis, brewer, who had caused himself to be technically assaulted by the Park-keeper with the view of raising the question. Court influence delayed the trial for three years, and when at length it came before the court, it would have been impossible to obtain a jury but for the spirited conduct of the judge, who fined absentees heavily, and got twelve men after waiting two hours. He showed the same determination in the hearing of the cause, sternly overruling the shifts and evasions of the Princess's lawyers, and the result was a verdict which established the popular right. Justice Foster, whose uprightness on this occasion has made him renowned, was an almost unique example of a judge who attained to the Bench by an almost exclusively provincial practice. Failing in Westminster Hall, he removed to Bristol, where he became recorder, and soon proved that, if not a great advocate, he possessed

The White Lodge, Richmond Park. Drawn by Clough Bromley.

the qualifications of a judge. The acumen he displayed in some decisions procured his promotion to the Court of King's Bench, which may have been assisted by his character as "a Whig of the old rock," as Horace Walpole calls him, and his nonconformist connections, the Duke of Newcastle, the premier of the day, always setting great store by the dissenting interest. His services to the public were not confined to this trial, for when, upon again going the circuit, Mr.

The White Lodge, Richmond Park, in the time of Lord Sidmouth.

Lewis complained that such a space had designedly been left between the steps of the ladder placed in consequence of the verdict that children and old men were unable to get up: "I have observed it myself," said the judge, "and I desire, Mr. Lewis, that you would see it so constructed that not only children and old men, but old women too, may be able to get up." In 1760, however, the right of carriage-way through the Park was decided at law against the inhabitants of Richmond. It is pleasing to add that when Lewis became embarrassed in his old age he was rescued from want by an annuity provided by public subscription at the instance of the incumbent of the parish, the Rev. Thomas Wakefield, brother of Gilbert Wakefield.

Only one important event has since occurred in the annals of Richmond Park, but it is one which will be always recorded in history. On June 23, 1894, a prince and presumptive heir to the crown of England was born to the Duke and Duchess of York at the White Lodge, situated within the precincts of the Park, and the residence of the Duke and Duchess of Teck, parents of the Duchess. In former times the Prince would probably have received the appellation of Edward of Richmond. Of the political importance of the event it is unnecessary to speak, and it is attended by a unique circumstance. "Never before has a child been born while its great grandmother was still occupying the throne of England."

White Lodge, where the royal birth occurred, was built about 1728 by George II., upon occasion of his making over the old lodge to Sir Robert Walpole. His queen, Caroline, and his daughter, Amelia, both lived here, and "The Queen's Drive," the long alley cut through the wood and leading up to the Park, is named after the former. The latter gave it up in disgust at the result of the Richmond Park trial. Lord Bute succeeded her as ranger in 1762, and the house is said to have fallen into decay, but this seems scarcely reconcilable with the statement that the wings were added in 1767. George III. improved it considerably when he bestowed it upon a favourite minister, Addington, afterwards Lord Sidmouth. Here Pitt visited Addington for the last time in 1805; and here, six weeks before Trafalgar, Nelson came to see him, and drew with wine on the table the plan by which he proposed to break the enemy's line, as he actually did. At a later period Queen Victoria retired here for a time, after the death of the Duchess of Kent. We give a view of the formal structure, fitter for Park Lane than for Richmond Park, as it appeared in Lord Sidmouth's time.

Another of the residences in the Park—Sheen Lodge—will be remembered after it shall have ceased to exist as a building, as the residence of Sir Richard Owen, the wonderful old man with whom few conversed without learning something that they did not know, and would have regretted not to have known. It was given by the

View from Richmond Hill.

Queen to Sir Richard Owen as a residence during his life, at the instance of the Prince Consort, and here he amused his last days with his garden and his favourite game of chess. In a map of 1754 the cottage is styled "The Dog Kennel," which leads to the conjecture that Sir Robert Walpole's kennels formerly stood there. On a similar ground, Pembroke Lodge, now indissolubly associated with the memory of Earl Russell, is believed to have been, in the eighteenth century, connected with mole-catching. Sir Richard Owen's house, originally

In Richmond Park looking towards Petersham.   Drawn by Clough Bromley.

the head keeper's lodge, was inhabited under the Regency by Governor Adam, the confidential friend of the Prince of Wales, who got up at Carlton House the dinner at which the Prince endeavoured to penetrate the secret of the Waverley Novels. It is now occupied by the Duke of Fife.

Many of the zoological attractions of the Park are now no more. Eels no longer migrate in countless shoals from the Pen Ponds (so called from being close by the pens where the deer were fed) to the river. Herons are comparatively infrequent. The graceful sylvan squirrels were destroyed for the same reason as the turkeys—the encouragement thus afforded to tramps and bad characters to infest the Park for the sake of killing and eating them! Our ruffians now expect better fare, and the squirrels might surely be reintroduced without much danger. The singing birds, however, are as of old, and continue to deserve the praise of Wordsworth, so generally known as a Lake Poet that it is almost forgotten that not his least productive period was passed in the south of England, and that many of his best poems are inspired by scenery and incidents south of the Humber :—

> Fame tells of groves—from England far away—
> Groves that inspire the Nightingale to trill
> And modulate with subtle reach of skill,
> Elsewhere unmatched, her ever-varying lay ;
> Such bold report I venture to gainsay :
> For I have heard the quire of Richmond Hill
> Chanting, with indefatigable bill,
> Strains that recalled to mind a distant day ;
> When, haply under shade of that same wood,
> And scarcely conscious of the dashing oars
> Plied steadily between those willowy shores,
> The sweet-souled Poet of the Seasons stood—
> Listening, and listening long, in rapturous mood,
> Ye heavenly Birds! to your Progenitors.

A fine sonnet, but for the grievous prosiness of the fifth line.

From the Park the transition to the Hill is natural. Perhaps there is no other eminence in the world which has obtained so wide and deserved a celebrity for the beauty of the prospect with such slender pretension on the score of elevation, abruptness, or boldness of natural features. Many circumstances have concurred to create this celebrity, above all, of course, the river, not only the loveliest of objects in itself, but the source of the surpassing verdure and richness of the scene. Leith Hill is far superior to Richmond Hill as an eminence, and the prospect is much more extensive, but the thirsty eye finds only a couple of ponds. The river from Richmond Hill must have varied greatly at different periods. The description of the land enclosed by Charles I. for the Park shows that it must have been for the most part ordinary Surrey common, most picturesque in the eye of the artist, but lacking most of the features now so indissolubly associated with Richmond that we almost assume that it must have been created with them. At a comparatively recent period the view

The Terrace, Richmond.   Drawn by Clough Bromley.

was much less rich than at present, but much more extensive. Thomson (about 1728) is especially impressed with its vastness :—

> Here let us sweep
> The boundless landscape ; now the raptured eye,
> Exulting, swift to huge Augusta send ;
> Now to the sister hills that skirt her plain ;
> To lofty Harrow now, and now to where
> Majestic Windsor lifts his princely brow.

View from Richmond Hill. By P. De Wint.

This enthusiasm seems rather overstrained in a poet fresh from Scotland. Milton, a Cockney and a Cantab, very probably had never seen a considerable hill when, living at Horton with his eye on Windsor Castle, "bosomed high in tufted trees," he sang of

> Mountains on whose barren breast
> The labouring clouds do often rest.

But if Thomson was magniloquent in his description of the boldness of the scenery he viewed, he was correct as to its extent. "Whoever," says Mr. Crisp, "will examine any one of the old engravings which represent the view from the terrace about a century or so since [before 1866] will observe that as the spectator stood to view the prospect, no matter which part of the hill he might select for so doing, there was scarcely a single tree, building, or otherwise, to impede a view down the river. There would not be any object whatever to prevent the eye ranging from the hills of Epsom, 'majestic Windsor,' round to the 'huge Augusta,' many of its lofty buildings being from the spot distinctly visible." What the landscape has lost in extent it has gained in richness; the balance of advantage and disadvantage is not easily struck, but it must be remembered that many of the former features of the scene which are now invisible wear a less attractive appearance at the present day than they did in the eighteenth century. The general character of the scene is well rendered in the following passage from the *British Angler's Manual* of T. C. Hofland, already mentioned as the painter of a celebrated picture of Richmond Hill :—" The placid stream presents on one side emerald turf of the finest texture and brightest verdure, lofty elms, interspersed with chestnuts, poplars, acacias, and all the lighter shrubs, shading noble mansions with hanging gardens, and elegant cottages; while on the other is seen the ancient village of Richmond, rising terrace-wise, and exhibiting every form of stately and of rural dwellings." Among the numerous travellers who have expressed their admiration of Richmond we may select the German Moritz (1782), who, combining literary ardour with passion for natural beauty, becomes, if possible, even too enthusiastic :—

"In every point of view," he says, "Richmond is assuredly one of the first situations in the world. Here it was that Thomson and Pope gleaned from nature all those beautiful passages with which their writings abound. Here I trod on the fresh, even, and soft verdure which is to be seen only in England; on one side of me lay a wood than which Nature cannot produce a finer, and on the other the Thames, with its shelvy bank and charming lawns rising like an amphitheatre, along which here and there one espies a picturesque white house, aspiring in majestic simplicity to pierce the dark foliage of surrounding trees, thus studding like stars in the galaxy the rich expanse of this charming vale. Sweet Richmond, never, no never shall I forget that lovely evening when from thy fairy hills thou didst so hospitably smile on me, a poor, lonely,

The View from Richmond Hill. By Turner. Reproduced from the Engraving by J. T. Wilmore, by T. Onson, R.P.E.

insignificant stranger. As I traversed to and fro thy meads, thy little swelling hills and flowery dells, and above all that queen of rivers thy own majestic Thames, I forgot all sublunary cares, and thought only of heaven and heavenly things. Happy, thrice happy am I, I again and again exclaimed, that I am here in Elysium!"

Before descending to the river, we may look at the Star and Garter, in its primitive form the subject of one of the illustrations in this

*Richmond Hill and the old Star and Garter. By J. D. Harding.
Engraved by T. Huson, R.P.E.*

monograph. The engraving is from a drawing by the antiquary Grose, preserved in the British Museum, which sufficiently indicates the humble beginnings of what has in our time been described as the most celebrated hotel in Britain. The hotel buildings are indicated by the sheds, as they appear, on the left hand, upon which the device of a Star and Garter can with some difficulty be made out. The inn was built in 1738, the year of the birth of George III. It was at first a mere house of entertainment; it was long, we are told, before it could undertake to provide a night's lodging for a tourist. Before 1780, however, it had become a two-storied house of some pretensions, and towards the end of the century it was greatly enlarged and improved by an enterprising landlord named

Brewer, who overshot the mark, and ended his days in a debtors' prison. After various vicissitudes, it entered in 1822, under the direction of Mr. Joseph Ellis, upon a career of prosperity only interrupted by its destruction by fire in 1870, which calamity merely occasioned its reconstruction upon a more sumptuous scale.

From the view the transition is easy to the river which forms its most attractive feature, and without which Richmond would not have existed as the abode of royalty or as the holiday resort of the people. The genealogy is unequivocal; the river made the Palace, the Palace made the Park, and the Park made the playground. During the Middle Ages we hear but little of the river. The various fishing weirs upon it are mentioned, chiefly in connection with the nobles and monasteries to whom they were at various times assigned, and there are numerous proofs of the importance of the ferry, which is probably older than the town. For nearly seven centuries this ferry satisfied the inhabitants of Richmond. An engraving after a picture by Marco Ricci, probably about 1720, represents a busy scene, frequented by pleasure-boats as well as the ferryman's humble craft; but towards the end of the third quarter of the eighteenth century a demand arose for a bridge. This the lessee of the ferry wished to build at his own expense, recouping himself by a toll; and prepared a design for a bridge with nine arches, partly stone and partly wood, a drawing of which is in the British Museum. The inhabitants, naturally enough, deemed such a structure deficient in solidity, and further objected to the suggested site at the place of the old ferry, on account of the inconvenience of the approach. Their arguments prevailed, and the existing bridge of five arches was built from the design of Messrs. Paine and Couse. Commenced in 1774, it was opened in December 1777. The expense of erection, about £26,000, was defrayed by money raised on the Tontine system, a kind of life annuity which ceases on the death of the last surviving shareholder. This did not occur until 1859, when the bridge was declared free of toll, and the gates were removed with much ceremony. The structure has always been admired, although the lines of the local laureate, the Rev. Thomas Maurice (1754-1824), a lazy, genial man of some repute as an Orientalist, who was at one time an assistant librarian of the British Museum, may be thought to err on the side of hyperbole :—

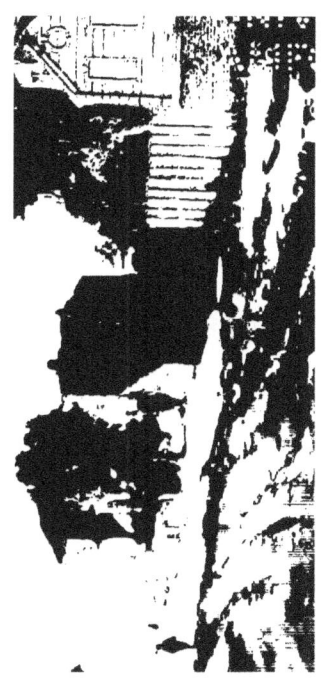

Richmond Bridge.

> Mark where yon beauteous Bridge with modest pride
> Throws its broad shadow o'er the subject tide—
> There Attic elegance and strength unite,
> And fair proportion's charms the eye delight ;
> There, graceful while the spacious arches bend,
> No useless, glaring ornaments offend—
> Embowered in verdure heaped unbounded round
> Of every varied hue that shades the ground,
> Its polished surface of unsullied white
> With heightened lustre beams upon the sight,
> Still lovelier in the shining flood surveyed
> Mid the deep masses of surrounding shade,
> Glittering with brilliant tints and burnished gold,
> Above, the cars of luxury are rolled,
> Or commerce, that upholds the wealthy thane,
> Guides to Augusta's towers her cumbrous wain ;
> Below, refulgent in the noontide ray,
> While in the breeze the silken streamers play,
> A thousand barks, arrayed in gorgeous pride,
> Bound o'er the surface of the yielding tide.

English poetry, taken as a whole, was probably never at a higher level of tumidity, or at a lower level of bathos, than when compositions like the above "petrifaction of a plodding brain," as Byron called the poem from which it is taken, were considered examples of correct taste, and poetasters like the Rev. T. Maurice shared public favour with Hayley and Erasmus Darwin.

Twickenham will come more appropriately into our concluding chapter, but some words may be given here to its islet, now so popularly known as Eel Pie Island, that it would be vain to seek to restore the proper designation of Twickenham Eyot. The great abundance of eels in the river in former days has been already mentioned, and they may probably have been deemed *de rigueur* at the picnics of which this pretty island, now graced with an inn, must have been the scene since the river has been dedicated to pleasure and enjoyment.

Nobler fish than eels were, until a comparatively recent period, among the boasts and delights of the Thames at Richmond and elsewhere. Could the mediæval denizens return, they would probably miss the Royal Palace much less than the salmon which in their day abounded in the waters ; the rather since the disappearance of the Palace is not unattended by compensations, but that of the salmon is unredeemed loss.

Steam navigation, the enormous growth of London, and the consequent obstruction of the lower reaches of the river by a mass of impurity, could not possibly have entered into their calculations; nor in their day were the hamlets which dotted the river-bank here and there, little towns contributing their quota to the general defilement, and permanently spoiling the river by the deposits of slimy ooze impregnated with sewage. As we write, a porpoise which was for some time in possession of the river between Hammersmith and Twickenham has been inhospitably destroyed by Messrs. Thornycroft's hands at Chiswick, but a salmon has not the constitution of a porpoise. The fish had become practically extinct by 1831, as appears from a conversation in Peacock's *Crotchet Castle*, published in that year.

Mr. Crotchet. That salmon before you, doctor, was caught in the Thames this morning.

The Rev. Dr. Folliott. Παπαπαί! Rarity of rarities! A Thames salmon caught this morning! Now, Mr. Mac Quedy, even in fish your Modern Athens must yield. *Cedite, Graii.*

Mr. Mac Quedy. Eh! sir, on its own ground, your Thames salmon has two virtues over all others: first, that it is fresh; and, second, that it is rare; for I understand you do not take half a dozen in a year.

The Rev. Dr. Folliott. In some years, sir, not one. Mud, filth, gas-dregs, lock-weirs, and the march of mind, developed in the form of poaching, have ruined the fishery. But, when we do catch a salmon, happy the man to whom he falls.

Mr. Hofland, writing in 1839, says: "Thirty years ago, at Mortlake, and between Isleworth and Richmond, I have seen from ten to twenty salmon taken at a draught; the last I saw caught in the Thames was in the year 1820, but they have been occasionally taken since that time." The ruin of the fishery, therefore, may be fixed as between 1810 and 1820, though no doubt it had long been declining. Though locks are disparaged in the passage from *Crotchet Castle* cited above, a word must be said in praise of the new lock below Richmond, which has saved the river from becoming a succession of mud-banks.

It is needless to add that those fish which do not ascend from the sea continue abundant in the Thames; few rivers, indeed, are more productive. The following passage from the chronicler Holinshed not only establishes the fecundity of the river in the sixteenth century, but is interesting as an indirect proof of its commercial value in that age. Now

The Ferry, with Richmond Lodge in the distance. After Marco Ricci. Engraved by T. Huson, R.P.E.

that the salmon have disappeared, and the other kinds of fish are but little eaten, netting is but rarely practised, angling has become a sport instead of a trade, and it is easier than it was in Holinshed's day to defend the river from "the insatiable avarice of the fishermen."

"This noble river, the Thames, yieldeth not clots of gold as the Tagus doth, but an infinite plentie of excellent, sweet, and pleasante fish, wherewith such as inhabit neere unto her banks are fed and fullie

The Duke of Buccleugh's Cottage, 1832; *now the Residence of Sir J. Whittaker Ellis, Bart. By G. Barnard. Engraved by T. Huson, R.P.E.*

nourished. What should I speake of the fat and sweet Salmon dailie taken in this streame, and that in such plentie after the time of the smelt be passed, and no river in Europe able to exceed it. What store of Barbels, Trouts, Pearches, Smelts, Breames, Roches, Daces, Gudgings, Flounders, Shrimps, etc., are commonlie to be had therein, I refer me to them that know by experience better than I by reason of their daily trade of fishery in the same; and albeit it seemeth from time to time to be, as it were, defrauded in sundrywise of these her large commodities by the insatiable avarice of the fishermen. Yet this famous river complaineth commonly of no want, but the more it looseth at one time the more it yieldeth at another. Onelie in carpes it seemeth to be scant, though it is not long since that kind of fish was brought to England. Oh that this river might be spared but even one yeare from nets! but alas! then shud manie a poore man be undone." The complaints of over-fishing were not new, for in the last year of Edward III. Parliament had petitioned the king to forbid certain kinds of engines, and nets below a certain width of mesh, and to exact a close time from January to May, which requests were complied with. Other petitions respected abuses alleged to exist concerning weirs, which proves the national importance attached to the Thames.

The house of Sir Joshua Reynolds, overlooking the river from the hill, has already been mentioned. The name of his great rival is also connected with Richmond, though not as a resident. "During the summer months," says Gainsborough's biographer Fulcher, "Gainsborough had lodgings at Richmond, and spent his mornings and evenings in sketching its very picturesque scenery. When in his walks he saw any peasant children that struck his fancy, he would send them to his painting-room, leaving with their parents very substantial proofs of his liberality. On one occasion he met with a boy named John Hill, on whom nature had bestowed a more than ordinary share of good looks, with an intelligence rarely found in a woodman's cottage. Gainsborough looked at the boy with a painter's eye, and, acting as usual on the impulse of the moment, offered to take him home and provide for his future welfare. Jack Hill was at once arrayed in his Sunday best, and sent with the gentleman, laden with as many virtuous precepts as would have filled a copy-book." After a brief trial, notwithstanding, Jack ran away, but not until he had been immortalised by the painter's pencil. Two portraits, one representing Jack warming his hands at a fire in a cottage, the other in a wood with a cat, are enumerated in Mr. Fulcher's catalogue of Gainsborough's works. The incident occurred not long before Gainsborough's death, after which Mrs. Gainsborough obtained Jack an admission to Christ's Hospital, where we lose sight of him. Gainsborough himself was buried at Kew, not from any local connection, but from his wish to be interred near his friend Joshua Kirby.

The name of another illustrious artist associated with this part of the

The Thames from the Duke of Buccleugh's Garden. By W. Westall, A.R.A. Engraved by T. Hnson, R.P.E.

Thames is that of Turner, whose views of Richmond Hill and Richmond Bridge are reproduced in this monograph. Turner, all his life a lover of the Thames, and who closed his eyes beside its waters at Chelsea, had lived at the Mall, Hammersmith, from 1808 to 1812, and in 1813 or 1814 purchased Sandycomb Lodge, Twickenham, where he remained until 1826. It is described by the Rev. Mr. Trimmer, in Mr. Thornbury's biography, as "an unpretending little place. There were several models of ships in glass cases, to which Turner had painted a sea and background. They much resembled the large vessels in his sea pieces. Richmond scenery greatly influenced his style. The Scotch firs (or stone-pine) around are in some of his large classical subjects, and Richmond landscape is decidedly the basis of 'The Rise of Carthage.' Here he had a long strip of land, planted by him so thickly with willows that his father, who delighted in the garden, complained that it was a mere osier-bed. Turner used to refresh his eye with the view of the boughs from his sitting-room window."

Here the great artist, except when absent on his foreign tours, spent his time painting assiduously, often from the boat which he kept upon the river; and occasionally amusing himself by fly-fishing. He would bring his captures home alive to put into a pond which he had himself dug in the garden, and was much annoyed by discovering that some mischievous person had introduced a pike. His aged father, the ex-barber of Covent Garden, always lived with him. Turner's filial piety is one of the most agreeable traits in his character; but the old gentleman partly earned his maintenance by varnishing his son's pictures, and going up daily to open the gallery in Queen Anne Street. Like his son he was parsimonious, and the expense weighed upon his mind until, as he related with glee, "I found out the inn where the market-gardeners baited their horses, I made friends with one on 'em, and now, for a glass of gin a day, he brings me up in his cart on the top of the vegetables."

79. *Thames and Twickenham Eyot.* By *T. M. Baynes, 1823. Engraved by T. Huson, R.P.E.*

CHAPTER IV

KEW—HAM—PETERSHAM—TWICKENHAM—STRAWBERRY HILL

To how many of the innumerable visitors to Kew has the inquiry suggested itself, Why Kew? What can be the origin of this queer little monosyllable? The name, rather Chinese than English in sound and physiognomy, and more in character by the banks of the Hoang Ho than those of the Thames, is at all events appropriately bestowed upon a place distinguished by a pagoda. When we find, however, that in the earliest records it is written "Kayhough," afterwards modified into "Kaiho" and "Kayo," it becomes clear that it has been formed by contraction from some longer word of less exotic appearance, and it may be conjectured that the last syllable had an affinity with "Hoe," as at Plymouth, and like this denoted a level by the waterside, while "Kay" may have been the name of some ancient proprietor, King Arthur's seneschal, if the reader pleases.

The vicinity of Kew to Richmond Palace naturally made it an appendage to the Court. The Earl of Worcester, Lord High Chamberlain to Henry VIII., had a residence here; and Leland, in a Latin poem, mentions a villa at *Cheva*, built by a steward of the Duke of Suffolk, who had married the king's sister, and lived at Suffolk Place hard by. In 1595 the Lord Keeper is found residing here, and entertaining Queen Elizabeth at dinner. The banquet was probably the least part of the expense, for the Keeper found it advisable to present Her Majesty with diamonds, artfully conveyed in fans and nosegays, to a considerable value, which the Queen so approved that "to grace his Lordship the more, she, of herself, took from him a salt, a spoon, and a fork of fair agate." Kew is not, however, named as a residence of any part of the royal family until 1730, when Frederick, Prince of Wales, took a lease of the property from the Capel family. Sir Henry, afterwards Lord, Capel (died 1696), even although Dr. Turner, the herbalist, is recorded to have had a garden of simples here in the reign of Edward VI., may be regarded as the original, though unintentional, founder of Kew Gardens, having created "an orangery and myrtetum" warmly commended by Evelyn. His evergreens are described in a pamphlet on gardens near London by J. Gibson, published in 1691. His connection and successor, Mr. Samuel Molyneux, was the first to give Kew a character in the other department of science for which it is celebrated, for he it was who placed in his own house, November 26, 1725, the telescope for the astronomer Bradley, by the aid of which his remarkable discovery of the aberration of light was made, December 17, 1725, though he did not succeed in finally working it out until September 1728, when the clue was given by the casual remark of a boatman on the river. The site is marked by a sun-dial erected by William IV. Prince Frederick naturally found it necessary to make very considerable alterations in the Capels' mansion, originally "a long building in the Italian style of architecture, very plain and uninteresting." The form which it ultimately assumed is shown in the drawings by Paul Sandby and Daniell, reproduced in our monograph. A "perspective view," taken apparently at an early period of his residence, and bound up with the splendid illustrated copy of Manning and Bray's *Surrey* in the British Museum, gives a lively idea of a very dead thing, the extreme formality of the plan of the grounds, which have, nevertheless, a certain congruity with the level, so uninteresting in itself, on which they are situated. Ground so liable to be overflowed must surely at one time have been a swamp, and must owe its redemption to forgotten heroes of the mediæval period, such as they who, probably about the time of Henry II., embanked the Essex shore of the Thames. The grounds were laid out by Kent, whose formal taste was shown not only in planning the gardens and plantations of the nobility about this time, but in the geometrical pavement of York Minster.

The history of Kew, in so far as it is connected with Prince Frederick, mainly concerns the unfortunate misunderstandings between him and his parents. The result was that when the prince was at Kew his residence was the centre of a little opposition Court, and was avoided

Richmond Bridge, from Isleworth Meadows. After R. R. Reinagle, R.A.

by all who wished to stand well with the king and queen. The prince's grand escapade of hurrying his wife to London within a few hours of her confinement, so graphically related by Lord Hervey, did not take place at Kew but at Hampton, and although his residence was a continual hotbed of intrigue, little to connect it either with national or with local history seems to have occurred there during his lifetime. A new era opens with the incumbency of his widow. This generally sensible and strong-

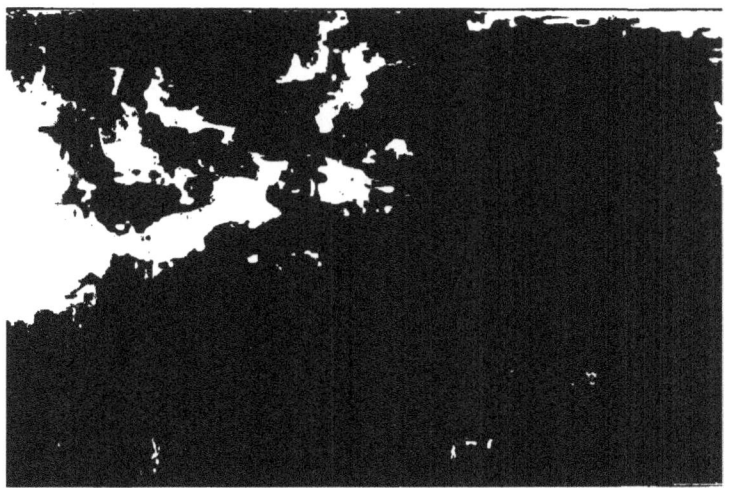

The Old Palace at Kew. By Paul Sandby, R.A.

minded woman was unable to forget her German antecedents, and place herself at the point of view of an English princess, and her influence upon her son, afterwards George III., is believed to have tended little to his own advantage or that of his kingdom. But in her connection with Kew she laid the nation under the greatest obligation, for from her proceeded the scientific impress which has given it its unique place among national possessions, and its supreme rank among the botanical institutions of the world. In 1759, the year in which the British Museum was opened to the public, the princess engaged William Aiton (chief gardener until his death in 1793, and compiler of the *Hortus Kewensis*) to establish a botanical, or, as it was then termed, a physic garden, which was laid out in the following year. In 1761 Sir William Chambers built for her what was then the largest greenhouse in the country, 114 feet in length. " A perpetual spring and summer ! " exclaims the Rev. S. Hales. " What a scene is here opened for improvements in greenhouse vegetation ! " The orangery was built in the same year. Even before the creation of the "physic garden" the grounds of Kew possessed great botanical importance, for in 1758 Sir John Hill was able to catalogue no fewer than 3400 species of trees, shrubs, flowers, and herbs " cultivated in the garden of H.R.H. the Dowager Princess of Wales at Kew." In 1761 numerous fine trees were transplanted to Kew from the grounds of the Duke of Argyle at Whitton ; and the great pagoda, 160 feet high and commanding a prospect of 40 miles circuit, was built in 1762. The garden had undoubtedly owed much to the taste and knowledge of the princess's favourite, the Earl of Bute, who was not only an able and scientific botanist, but made botany, apart from politics, the principal occupation of his life.[1] He became Groom of the Stole to the young Prince of Wales on the death of his father, and his official residence kept him continually upon the spot. He had a fine botanical library and collection of dried plants, and was himself the author, or at least the publisher, of *Botanical Tables*, " opus splendidum magis quam utile," says Sir Joseph Banks's librarian Dryander. Only twelve copies were printed, one of which sold for as much as £120. An account of the buildings and gardens at Kew was published in 1763 by Sir William Chambers, in which he says : " The Physic or Exotic Garden cannot possibly be yet in its perfection, but from the great botanical learning of him who is the principal manager [Lord Bute], and the assiduity with which all curious productions are collected from every part of the globe, without any regard to expense, it may be concluded that within a few years this will be the amplest and best collection of curious plants in Europe." Bute also took an important part in the improvement of the grounds. " The gardens of Kew," says Sir William Chambers, " are not very large, nor is their situation by any means

---

[1] It may be added that it was also the cause of his death, for he died in consequence of injuries received in climbing after a rare plant on a cliff near Christchurch.

advantageous; as it is low and commands no prospects. Originally the ground was one continued dead flat, the soil was in general barren, and without either wood or water. With so many disadvantages, it was not easy to produce anything tolerable in gardening; but princely munificence, guided by a director equally skilled in cultivating the earth and in the polite arts, overcame all difficulties. What was once a desert is now an Eden."

The princess died in 1772. George III. bought the freehold, and maintained the botanical character of the place with even more energy than his mother, but Lord Bute disappeared, and Sir Joseph Banks reigned in his stead. We shall return to Kew Gardens, but the royal establishment claims first notice.

George III. was partial to Kew from his affection for his mother, and as the place where his infancy and boyhood had been spent. He had further cause to remember Kew Green as the spot where, riding to London to give directions for the construction of an organ, he had been met by a private messenger bearing news of the death of his grandfather and his consequent accession to the crown. With the reserve which always characterised him, he turned back, sent his horse to the stable, and, enjoining silence on his attendant, awaited the official communication. After his mother's death he resided as much as possible at Kew Palace between May and November. It is well known how plain and homely was the life he there led with his consort. "Their Majesties," says Mrs. Delany, "rise at six, and call two hours their own. At eight the Prince of Wales and the Bishop of Osnaburgh [known to history as the Duke of York] with the princesses come to breakfast. Then the elder ones work, and the little ones are taken by their nurses to the royal gardens. In the afternoon the queen works, and the king reads to her. Once a week the king and queen, with their whole family in pairs, make the tour of the gardens. In the evening the children again pay their duty before they go to bed." This routine, however, did not exclude amusements, but always of a sober cast; and it can scarcely be wondered that the princes indemnified themselves when they at last obtained access to London society. As boys they seem to have enjoyed themselves, working with their own hands in the gardens, and growing wheat, which they ground and baked and presented to their parents. Fanny Burney's lively picture of an exceedingly dull life, both at Windsor and Kew, is too well known to require quotation. She complains bitterly of the inconvenience of the old palace, which would scarcely have been inhabited by a monarch of less homely tastes than George III. It afforded him an asylum during his temporary insanity in 1788-89, when, says Miss Burney pathetically, "the master of the house was not its owner." After the king's recovery he continued to reside at Kew, but at length (1803) pulled down the old palace as he had done the far superior edifice of Queen Caroline at Richmond. He replaced it by a castellated mansion on the bank of the river, which did not prove a success. The situation, immediately opposite Brentford, was disadvantageous, and the views, which are all that remain of it, show that it was but a poor specimen of Wyatt's pseudo-Gothic. "Though still unfinished," says Wraxall, "unfurnished, and uninhabited, as it will probably ever remain, it presents to the eye an assemblage of towers and turrets, forming a structure such as those in which Ariosto or Spenser depicture princesses detained by giants or enchanters." Sir Richard Phillips (1817) "could not conceive the motive for preferring an external form which rendered it impracticable to construct within it more than a series of large closets, boudoirs and rooms with oratories." George IV. pulled it down in 1828. While it was building, the old palace having been demolished, the royal family, when at Kew, resided in a house which has survived all the rest, and still bears the name of palace, the so-called Old Dutch House, a misnomer, since it is a Jacobean mansion bearing date 1631. Here Queen Charlotte died in 1818, but her presence in Kew at the time was accidental.

So active had George III.'s encouragement of botany been, that upwards of six thousand trees, shrubs, and plants of all descriptions are stated to have been introduced into England during his reign. He owed much to the constant assistance of Sir Joseph Banks, who was accused, and probably with justice, of illiberality towards other botanists and collectors, but who at all events, without any official position or pecuniary inducement, devoted time and money without stint to make Kew the first botanical garden in the world. The number of collectors sent out to all parts of the world during his administration, and

Kew Gardens in the Eighteenth Century. By W. Woollett.

enumerated in the present director's, Mr. Thiselton Dyer's invaluable " Historical Account of Kew to 1841 " (*Kew Bulletin*, December 1891) sufficiently proves the vigour with which affairs were then carried on. After George III.'s hopeless insanity in 1810, Kew, as Mr. Thiselton Dyer expresses it, went downhill for thirty years. George IV. and William IV., indeed, occasionally evinced a spasmodic interest. The former, when Regent, thought of establishing a library there; and the latter, shortly after his accession, expressed regret that he was too old to

Palace at Kew built by George III. By W. Daniell, R.A.

build on the spot. But no collectors were sent out under the reign of either, though something had been done under George IV. as Regent. It may be significant that the period of his accession as king nearly corresponded with the death of Sir Joseph Banks. It should be added that during the whole of this period the Gardens were more or less open to the public.

After the death of William IV. Professor Lindley was directed by the Government to make an inquiry in conjunction with two practical gardeners into the state of the Botanic Garden. His report was not in general very favourable, although he admitted the excellence of the Australian collections. For some reason this report was not presented to Parliament until May 1840, when the fate of the Garden had been already determined. In 1839 alarming reports were circulated that it was intended to break the Garden up altogether, and to divide the plants between the Royal Horticultural Society and the Royal Botanical Society. The Lord Steward, it was said, proposed to convert the Botanic Garden into "vineries and pine-stoves." It was added that the Council of the Horticultural Society had received and declined an offer of plants. These reports excited much indignation, manifested by articles in the press; and the Government, called to account by Lord Aberdeen in March 1840, denied the existence of any such intention on their part, and hastened to give the best evidence of their sincerity by transferring the Gardens from the Lord Chamberlain's department to the department of Woods and Forests, thus rendering them virtually public property. It is believed that the interference of Her Majesty and the Prince Consort had much to do with this fortunate decision, which started the Gardens upon a new career of energetic usefulness, and such an extension of space and development of attraction for the public as had never been dreamed of even in the golden days of George III. Since then there have been three directors, Sir William Jackson Hooker, Sir Joseph Dalton Hooker, and Mr. Thiselton Dyer. The two latter are living. Of Sir William Hooker (1841-65) it is sufficient to record that under him "a garden of 11 acres was extended to 75 acres of botanic garden, and 270 acres of arboretum and pleasure-ground, and ten old conservatories and hothouses were replaced by twenty-five houses of modern construction and considerably greater size. His herbarium, by far the richest ever accumulated in one man's lifetime, was after his death purchased by the nation. By his enormous correspondence and prompt acknowledgment of assistance he maintained friendly relations with the Indian and Colonial governments, which in their turn reaped lasting benefits from the distribution of plants from Kew" (*Dictionary of National Biography*).

Apart from royalty and the Botanic Garden, Kew may claim celebrity as the abode of many distinguished persons, especially artists. Sir Peter Lely's house was on the site of the present herbarium. A still greater painter, Gainsborough, long lived and was ultimately interred here, near his friends Meyer the miniaturist, and Zoffany, an excellent portrait painter. The reputation of Francis Bauer, draughtsman to the Royal Gardens (*d.* 1840), is most strictly local, but still very high. Niepce's experiments in photography were made at Kew in 1827 under his countenance, and with most liberal support from the Royal Society,

Kew Green. Drawn by Clough Bromley.

then at a low ebb of usefulness, might have anticipated the discovery of Daguerre. Among eminent residents may be named two oddly contrasted people, Mrs. Trimmer, the mentor of British youth, and the Reverend Caleb Colton, author of *Lacon* and incumbent of the chapel from 1818 to 1828, when too little residence and too much gambling led to his deprivation.

The three Hams remain for notice, Petersham, Ham, and Twickenham. Of Petersham there is not much to be said, although it is the oldest of all the places commemorated in this sketch, being mentioned in Domesday Book. It appears as an offshoot from the Abbey of

Chertsey, and derives its name from the saint to whom the abbey was dedicated. In the time of William the Conqueror the fishery was estimated to produce 1000 eels and 1000 lamperns annually. The monastery must have enjoyed a considerable reputation for sanctity if we are correctly informed by Aubrey that Petersham at one time enjoyed the privilege that no person could be arrested in it, and no person already under arrest brought through it, which privilege was

Petersham Church. Drawn by Clough Bromley.

lost by what Aubrey, to whom it would at divers times have been singularly convenient, considers "scandalous neglect." In Henry V.'s reign the monks conveyed their rights in Petersham parish to the king, and were probably incorporated into one of his religious foundations at Richmond. There seems no other incident of interest in the history of Petersham, except that it was granted by Henry VIII. to his repudiated wife, Anne of Cleves. Petersham Lodge, an imposing fabric, was built about 1722 from the designs of Lord Burlington, to replace an older mansion consumed by a fire which is said to have destroyed many MSS. of Lord Chancellor Clarendon. After many vicissitudes of ownership, it was sold in 1834 to the Woods and Forests, and pulled down. Sudbrook Park, a neighbouring seat where Canning once lived, and where the Reform Bill is said to have been drafted during the tenancy of Lord Durham, after a transition stage as a hydropathic establishment, has become a hotel. Among distinguished residents at Petersham may be named Gay's Duchess of Queensberry and her poet, who possessed a summer-house here which

Ham House. Drawn by Clough Bromley.

boatmen are said to have been in the habit of palming off as Thomson's upon unwary voyagers. The sisters Berry, noticed in our second chapter, are interred at Petersham.

Ham House is in Petersham parish, although its name connects it more nearly with the ancient hamlet of Ham. Built by Sir Thomas Vavasour in 1610, it came into the possession of the Duke of Lauderdale and his still more celebrated duchess, "a woman of great beauty and greater parts," says the antagonistic Burnet, and achieved undying historical notoriety as the reputed place of the meetings of the Cabal in Charles II.'s time. A few years after the dissolution of the Cabal

Ministry it is described by Evelyn as "inferior to few of the best villas in Italy itself; the house furnished like a great prince's; the parterres, flower gardens, orangéries, groves, avenues, courts, statues, perspectives, fountains, aviaries, and all this at the banks of the sweetest river in the world, must needs be admirable." When, however, ten years afterwards, James II. was urged to go into honourable captivity here, His Majesty discovered that Ham was "a very ill winter house, being damp and unfurnished." It is now pronounced "rather curious than fine," but holds a high place among the historical houses of England for its sets of apartments, those occupied by the Duchess of Lauderdale remaining precisely as she left them; for its library with fourteen Caxtons and other treasures; for its original MS. documents of the time of Charles II. and James II.; and for its portraits, many by Vandyke and Lely.

Returning to the river, we find our way to Twickenham lined with memorable houses, full of historical association. Syon House, which Somerset began to build on the site of the suppressed convent, passed from him to his supplanter Northumberland, and remains in the Duke of Northumberland's family to this day. Its striking appearance from the river is familiar to all. Still more interest would attach, did it now exist, to an adjoining mansion once the property of Bacon, and pulled down in the present century, after undergoing changes of ownership which recall the epigram in the Greek Anthology :—

> Cleon's I was, to Cleitophon was sold;
> Another's soon; soon will another hold
> What each calls his, but, the pure truth to say,
> Fortune's I am and I shall be alway.

Cambridge House, with its reminiscences of the accomplished owner in last century, Johnson's friend, and of Johnson himself; Marble Hill, where the Marquis Wellesley resided for a time; Orleans House, long in the occupation of Louis Philippe as an exile, and afterwards, when the wheel of change had made another circuit, of the Duc d'Aumale; are the chief mansions along the river-bank to Twickenham, two of whose classic residences demand a fuller notice. Pope's Villa, indeed, though still existing in name, has vanished from the earth, while Strawberry Hill remains; but the fame of Twickenham is much more intimately associated with the former. After Stratford-on-Avon and the Lake country, indeed, it would hardly be easy to discover a place or district in England more intimately associated with the name of a great author than Twickenham is with Pope's.

In 1718 Pope's imagination had been much occupied with plans for building and planting during his residence with Lord Bathurst, and in 1719 he invested a portion of the proceeds of his translation of Homer in the purchase, from a Turkey merchant named Vernon, of the long lease of a house and a few acres of land—"a little bit of ground of five acres," says Horace Walpole, "enclosed with three lanes, and seeing nothing." Pope twisted and twirled and rhymed and harmonised this till it appeared two or three sweet little lawns opening and opening beyond one another, and the whole surrounded with thick impenetrable woods. "The grounds," says Mr. Courthope, "were ultimately made to comprise a shell temple, a large mount, two small mounts, a bowling-green, a quincunx, an obelisk in memory of the poet's mother, as well as hot-houses and gardeners' sheds." The famous grotto, which performed the useful part of connecting the house with the grounds which had formerly been divided from it by a road, was made in the following year. "Pope," says Dr. Johnson, "extracted an ornament from an inconvenience, and vanity produced a grotto where necessity forced a passage." There is an eloquent description of this grotto in a letter from Pope to Blunt (No. 16 in Elwin's edition), in which he speaks of the happy effect of seeing from it "the sails in the river passing suddenly and vanishing as through a perspective glass." He is also proud of its sparkling effect when lighted up, a feature owing at the time to nothing more exceptional than the insertion in the wall of pieces of looking-glass. Not long before his death, however, says Warburton, he had "incrusted it with a great number of ores and minerals of the richest and rarest kinds," a statement confirmed by the views and curious account of it published shortly after his death by his gardener Serle. Among the minerals there mentioned are silver ore from Mexico, gold ore from Peru, "Cornish diamonds," amethysts, bloodstones, and "some very particular sorts of fossils." Many of them are mentioned as the gifts of friends. If the taste thus displayed seems somewhat childish, the same cannot be said of Pope's taste in laying out his miniature grounds, which actually, perhaps too anxiously, attempted

Pope's House, Twickenham. From an old Engraving.

the imitation of Nature, and conformed to Pope's own precepts in his verse. It is remarkable that he whose versification was so balanced and artificial, should have been pleased with irregularity in landscape, and denounced the formality through which

> Grove nods to grove, each alley has its brother,
> And half the garden but reflects the other.

It was but natural that his ideas should have failed to commend themselves to his successors in the property. In 1760 Sir William Stanyer made alterations which drew upon him the objurgations of Horace Walpole, and the villa was pulled down about 1807 by the then possessor, Lady Howe, who thereby earned the title of "Queen of the Goths." The new villa which arose in its stead was known as Pope's, and less reverently as the Tea-caddy. It was not his, nor is it on the site of his; although the celebrity it has acquired as the residence of a distinguished politician from Northampton may remind us that Pope's villa too was a centre of politics during the disputes between George II. and his son Frederick, Prince of Wales, and that conclaves of the latter's friends were frequently held there.

"All," says Mr. Cobbett in his *Memorials of Twickenham*, "that Twickenham has preserved of her greatest resident is, in the church, a grave wherein his remains rest, impenetrably sealed up, and all traces of its exact site entirely hidden from view; two words on a tablet, and a date; and last of all, a monument remarkable for the pre-eminent bad taste of its inscription; from this, during the restoration of the church in 1859, the whole of its marble laurel wreath was chipped off bit by bit by wretches who wanted to possess a piece of *Pope's tomb*. Outside the church nothing remains but his grotto, now despoiled of most of its former adornments." Another illustrious poet, Tennyson, lived at Twickenham in 1851 and 1852; but no record of his residence seems to remain beyond the account of a visit paid him there by William Allingham.

We give a view of Twickenham Church, which has numbered two eminent men among its vicars—Waterland, the celebrated writer on the Trinity, and Terrick, Bishop of London from 1764 to 1777.

As daybreak is sometimes preceded by a false appearance of dawn,

so the genuine romantic revival of the latter part of the eighteenth century was preceded by a premonitory symptom in a taste for sham Gothic, appearing first in the region of human effort where the spell of Gothic was most potent, namely, in architecture, and thence extending to literature. This dilettante yet not insincere taste is personified in a building and a book, both creations of the same mind—Horace Walpole's Gothic villa at Strawberry Hill, and his *Castle of Otranto*. The villa

Strawberry Hill. By Paul Sandby, R.A. Engraved by T. Huson, R.P.E.

is not good architecture and the book is not good literature, yet neither can be omitted from the history of culture. Walpole himself, it need not be said, was much more than a dilettante architect or romancer. He seems to have been created to be the mirror of his age in its social and therefore some of its most frivolous aspects; but if his tastes were individually trifling and his talents individually petty, the aggregate was more than respectable. In former days Strawberry Hill afforded a visible representation of the character of its creator which, since the dispersal of his collections, we must seek in his writings. "In his villa," writes

Macaulay, "every apartment is a museum; every piece of furniture is a curiosity; there is something strange in the form of the shovel; there is a long story belonging to the bell-rope." Carrying out the parallel between the collections and the collector, Macaulay, whose general estimate of Walpole appears to us too low, admits that "no man who has written so much is so seldom tiresome"—a compliment, we

The Gallery, Strawberry Hill. From an old Engraving. Reproduced by T. Huson, R.P.E.

may add, equally appropriate to Macaulay himself. The world has now made up its mind about sham Gothic; and instead of criticising this famous house from a nineteenth-century point of view, let us rather profit by the statement of a contemporary writer (Miss Pye: *A Short Account of the Principal Seats and Gardens in and about Twickenham*) that "Mr. Walpole's house represents an ancient abbey, and the inside is quite answerable to its venerable aspect." Within, the lady's attention seems to have been chiefly attracted by a remarkable bed, but she adds: "The windows are all painted, and so exquisitely, that they seem to promise a revival of this long-forgotten art. The library contains a fine collection of books, and is entirely calculated for learned retirement and contemplation. You are struck with awe at entering it." The pretty booklet from which this extract is taken has been conjectured to have been printed at the Strawberry Hill Press, but does not appear in Mr. H. B. Wheatley's catalogue of its productions in *Bibliographica*, and it can hardly be believed that "the fastidious amateur" would have passed so many eccentricities in orthography. This press, established in 1757 at an adjoining house, was a constant source of trouble and expense to Walpole, but, although many of its productions were trifling or occasional, others do him much honour. Of the *genius loci* himself, Mr. Wheatley observes with justice: "He was considered effeminate in his own day because he devoted himself to the collection of things of beauty with great taste and judgment, but now his prescience is justified. The sale at Strawberry Hill in 1842 created a great sensation, but in 1896 it would create a still greater one, and the contents of Walpole's 'castle' would now probably sell for at least four times as much as the thirty-three thousand pounds then realised." Would, then, the china bowl in which "the pensive Selima," immortalised by Gray, found a watery grave, which then produced £42, now produce £168? As admirers of the feline species, we hope so.

The origin of Strawberry Hill was sufficiently humble; it arose out of a lodging-house built in 1698 by a coachman of the Earl of Bradford. It must soon have been enlarged, having between 1720 and 1730 served as a summer retreat for that princely prelate, Talbot, Bishop of Durham, who was followed by the Marquis of Carnarvon. Walpole acquired the "rural bijou," as he calls it, in 1747, and set himself to remodel it, so as to give it the venerable air which so impressed Miss Pye thirteen years afterwards. "Whatever," observes Mr. Chancellor, "may be said about the trumperiness or defective taste exhibited in 'The Castle,' as Walpole delighted to call it, it had one merit, that of consistency. Everything was in keeping, the internal arrangements and the external decorations were all Gothic—Gothic of a filigree nature if you will, but still Gothic." At Walpole's death he left the house to his cousin Marshal Conway and the Countess of Ailesbury during their lives, and then to their daughter, Mrs. Damer, who lived there until 1828, when she removed to York House, now the residence of Sir Mountstuart Grant Duff, and Strawberry Hill passed to Lord Waldegrave. After the sale in 1842 the late gifted and popular Countess of Waldegrave made it again a brilliant resort during her life; it is now the property of Baron Stern. The very charms of the district we have been describing, and the temptation afforded to successive generations to fix their habitations in it, have conduced to more rapid and frequent changes of ownership, and consequent renovations, dilapidations, and obliterations, than the scourges of war and revolution have effected in less favoured lands. Such will ever be the case so long as the Thames, regardless of the ennui of the Duke of Queensberry, continues to "flow, flow, flow," provided that the stream of national prosperity continues to flow with it.

INDEX

Aberdeen, Lord, 89
Adam, Governor, 57
Addington (Lord Sidmouth), 56
Ailesbury, Countess of, 102
Aiton, William, 83
Allingham, William, 96
Amelia, Princess 52
Anne of Bohemia, 8
Anne of Cleves, 19, 91
Anne, Queen, 24, 29
Argyle, Duke of, 84
Arran, Earl of, 29
Arthur, Prince of Wales, 16
Aubrey, 25, 91
d'Aumale, Duc, 93

Banks, Sir Joseph, 84-87
Bathurst, Lord, 94
Bauer, Francis, 90
Baynes, Adam, 24
Belet, John, 7
Bergenroth, Mr., 12
Berners, Lady, 8
Berry, the Misses, 45, 92
Boleyn, Anne, 18, 19
Bradley (astronomer), 80
British Museum, 65, 66, 80, 83
Brouncker, Henry, 28
Buchan, Lord 38
Burlington, Lord, 91
Burney, Fanny, 86
Bute, Lord, 56, 84, 85

Cambridge House, 93
Camden, William, 7
Canning, 92
Capel, Lord, 80
Carlisle, Earl of, 45
Carnarvon, Marquis of, 101
Caroline, Queen, 29, 33-36, 56, 86
Castlemaine, Lady, 50
Catherine of Aragon, 10, 16, 19
Chambers, Sir William, 46, 84

Chancellor, Mr., 35, 101
Charles I., 18, 21, 22, 24, 33, 49, 50, 52, 58
Charles II., 5, 28, 50
Charles V., The Emperor, 19
Charlotte, Queen, 86
Cholmondeley, Earl of, 42
Cibber, Colley, 35, 47
Colet, Dean, 19
Collins, William, 39
Colton, Caleb, 90
Compton, Sir Spencer, 30
Conway, Marshal, 102
Cottington, Francis, 49
Courthope, Mr., 94
Crisp, Mr., 12, 45, 61

Damer, Mrs., 102
Daniell, W., 80
Delany, Mrs., 85
Disraeli, Benjamin, 47
Duck, Stephen, 35
Durham, Lord, 92
Dyer, Mr. Thiselton, 88, 89
Dysart, Lord, 49

Edward I., 7
Edward II., 8
Edward III., 8, 74
Edward IV., 8, 9
Edward VI., 19, 25, 80
Eel Pic Island, 69
Eisenberg (traveller), 18
Elizabeth, Queen, 5, 18-21, 25, 79
Elmham, 8
Errol, Lord, 18
Evelyn, John, 28, 29, 80, 93

Fagniani, Maria, 42
Fife, Duke of, 57
Foster, Justice, 52
Frederick, Prince of Wales, 34, 80, 96
Fulcher, Rev. Thos., 74
Fuller, 24

Gainsborough, Thomas, 74
Gay, John, 92
George II., 29, 33, 36, 50, 51, 56, 96
George III., 35, 56, 65, 83, 85, 86, 88, 89
George IV., 85, 86, 88
Gerschen, Friedrich, 17, 18
Goodwin, William, 24
Grasser (traveller), 18
Gray, Thomas, 101
Greenwich, 5
Grose (antiquary), 12, 65
Gwynne, Nell, 5

Ham, 90
Ham House, 92, 93
Hampton Court, 15, 18, 19, 27, 28
Henrietta Maria, 24
Henry, Prince of Wales, 21
Henry I., 7
Henry II., 80
Henry III., 7
Henry IV., 8, 25
Henry V., 8, 25, 91
Henry VI., 8
Henry VII., 5, 8, 9, 12, 15, 16, 17, 23, 26
Henry VIII., 17, 18, 79, 91
Hervey, Lord, 30, 33, 35, 36, 83
Hill, Jack, 74
Hill, Sir John, 84
Hofland, Barbara, 45
Hofland, T. C., 46, 62, 70
Holbein, 28, 35
Holinshed, 70
Hollar, Wenceslas, 16
Hooker, Sir J. D., 89
Hooker, Sir W. J., 96
Howe, Lady, 93

James IV. of Scotland, 25
James VI. of Scotland, 21
Jesse, Mr., 49
Johnson, Dr., 39, 45, 93, 94
Juxon, Bishop, 49

INDEX

Kean, Edmund, 46, 47
Kent, Duchess of, 56
Kent (architect), 80
Kew, 6, 34, 74, 79, 80-90

Langton, Bennet, 45
Langton, Miss Mary, 45
Laud, Archbishop, 49
Lauderdale, Duchess of, 92, 93
Lauderdale, Duke of, 92
Leicester, Earl of, 28
Leland (poet), 79
Lely, Sir Peter, 90, 93
Lewis, John, 52
Lindley, Professor, 88
Lisle, Lord, 28
Louis Philippe, 93

Macaulay, 29, 100
Magalotti, 28
Marble Hill, 93
Martin, Lady, 47
Mary, Queen, 19, 20, 25, 27
Mary, Queen of Scots, 21
Matthew of Westminster, 7
Maurice, Rev. Thomas, 66, 67
Metternich, 47
Meyer, William, 96
Mitford, Miss, 46
Molyneux, Samuel, 80
Moor Park, 29
Moritz, 62
Mortlake, 49

Nelson, 56
Newcastle, Duke of, 52
Niepce, 90
Northumberland, Earl of, 93
Norton, Sir Gregory, 24

Orford, Earl of, 51, 52
Orleans House, 93
Ormond, Duke of, 29
Osnaburg, Bishop of, 85
Owen, Sir Richard, 57

Parker, Sir James, 9
Pepys, 28
Perrers, Alice, 8
Petersham, 25, 45, 90, 91, 92
Petersham Lodge, 91
Philip II., 19

Philip of Castile, 16
Pomerania, Duke of, 17
Pope, Alexander, 62, 93-96
Portland, Earl of, 50
Prince Consort, The, 57, 89
Puebla, De, 12
Pye, Miss, 100, 101

Queensberry, Duchess of, 92
Queensberry, Duke of, 41, 42, 102
Quin, 38

Reynolds, Sir Joshua, 40, 41, 74
Ricci, Marco, 66
Richard II., 8
Richmond Court. *See* Richmond Palace
Richmond Hill, 6, 7, 58
Richmond Lodge, 19, 33, 35, 36
Richmond Palace, 12-24
Richmond Theatre, 47
Robsart, Amy, 25
Rookesby, Thomas, 24
Rye, W. B., 18

Saint Bridget's Nunnery, 25, 26
Sandby, Paul, 80
Scott, Sir Walter, 36
Seymour, Jane, 19
Sheen *or* Shene, 7-10, 12, 29
Sheen Lodge, 56
Shene Chase, 49
Shene Friary, 25, 26
Shene Priory, 25, 28
Somerset, Protector, 93
Somerset House, 33
Stanyer, Sir William, 96
Star and Garter Hotel, 65
Stephen, King, 7
Stern, Baron, 102
Strawberry Hill, 93, 99-102
Strype, 24
Sudbrook Park, 92
Suffolk, Duke of, 79
Suffolk, Lady, 34
Swift, Jonathan, 29
Syon Convent, 7
Syon House, 7, 25, 93

Talbot, Bishop of Durham, 101

Teck, Duke and Duchess of, 56
Temple, Sir William, 25, 28, 29
Tennyson, 96
Terrick, Bishop, 96
Thackeray, 30
Thomson, James, 6, 36-39, 61, 62, 92
Trimmer, Mrs., 90
Turner, J. W. M., 76
Turner, Dr., 80
Tuscany, Grand Duke of, 28
Twickenham, 69, 76, 90, 93-96

Vandyke, 93
Vaughan, Hugh, 9
Vavasour, Sir Thomas, 92
Victoria, Queen, 56, 57, 89
Villiers, Edward, 24
Villiers, Lady Frances, 24
Vinckenboom, 16

Wakefield, Gilbert, 56
Wakefield, Rev. Thomas, 56
Waldegrave, Lady, 102
Waldegrave, Lord, 102
Walpole, Horace, 35, 45, 50, 51, 94, 99-101
Walpole, Sir Robert, 30, 33, 51, 52, 56, 57
Warbeck, Perkin, 25
Waterland (divine), 96
Wellesley, Marquis, 93
Wheatley, H. B., 101
White Lodge, 56
Whitton, 84
Wick House, 40
William III., 29
William IV., 80, 87
Wolsey, Cardinal, 15, 19, 27
Woodville, Elizabeth, 8
Wordsworth, 39
Worcester, Earl of, 79
Wraxall, Sir N., 86

Yarmouth, Lord, 45
York, Richard, Duke of, 8
York, Duke of (James II.), 23, 24
York, Duke of (Prince George), 56

Zingerling (traveller), 18
Zoffany, 96

Printed by R. & R. Clark, Limited, *Edinburgh.*

www.ingramcontent.com/pod-product-compliance
Lightning Source LLC
Chambersburg PA
CBHW020145170426
43199CB00010B/897